BY FOREST WAYS IN NEW ZEALAND

BY FOREST WAYS IN NEW ZEALAND

F. A. ROBERTS

ISBN: 978-93-5614-364-7

Published: -

LECTOR HOUSE LLP

LECTOR HOUSE

LECTOR HOUSE LLP
E-MAIL: lectorpublishing@gmail.com

COLOURED BERRIES OF SUPPLE JACK.

Frontispiece.

BY FOREST WAYS IN NEW ZEALAND

BY

F. A. ROBERTS

CONTENTS

Chapter   *Page*

I. WELLINGTON 1

II. STEWART ISLAND 5

III. OVERLAND TO MILFORD SOUND .9

IV. THE COLD LAKES OF OTAGO 17

V. THE NEW ZEALAND EDINBURGH 21

VI. AMONG THE SOUTHERN ALPS 24

VII. CHRISTCHURCH 31

VIII. FROM CHRISTCHURCH TO THE WEST COAST 35

IX. THREE WEEKS IN WESTLAND 41

X. THROUGH THE BULLER VALLEY 48

XI. THE COPLAND PASS 52

XII. THE WESTLAND GLACIERS 59

XIII. THE WAITOMO CAVES 70

XIV. NEW ZEALAND'S WONDERLAND 74

XV. AUCKLAND 81

LIST OF ILLUSTRATIONS

Page

I. COLOURED BERRIES OF SUPPLE JACK. iv

II. A SANDY COVE—STEWART ISLAND. 7

III. CLINTON RIVER—TE ANAU LAKE. 10

IV. LAKE WAKATIPU. 16

V. OTAGO HARBOUR. 22

VI. ROAD BETWEEN FAIRLIE AND THE HERMITAGE. 25

VII. MOUNT COOK LILIES. 28

VIII. RIVER AVON AT CHRISTCHURCH IN WINTER. 32

IX. THE WESTLAND FOREST. .39

X. FRANZ JOSEF AND ALMER GLACIERS FROM CAPE DEFIANCE.. . 44

XI. MOUNTS SEFTON AND FOOTSTOOL FROM COPLAND PASS. . . .54

XII. GLACIER HOTEL, WAIHO GORGE. 58

XIII. ICE PINNACLES, ALMER GLACIER. 61

XIV. MOUNT MOLTKE AND VICTORIA GLACIER FROM CHAN-
CELLOR RIDGE.. 65

XV. SOUTHERN ALPS FROM MOUTH OF WAIHO RIVER.. 68

XVI. LAKE ROTORUA.. 75

XVII. MAORI ANCESTRAL FIGURE. 82

BY FOREST WAYS IN NEW ZEALAND

CHAPTER I

WELLINGTON

The ship which brought me to New Zealand called first at Wellington, the capital city, with a population, as I afterwards heard, of ninety thousand.

Ships steam up a narrow, rocky channel into the harbour, which widens out into an area of fifty square miles, with deep water right up to the town, and wharves adjoining the chief streets. All round the harbour are hills, most of them now cleared of trees and grass-grown; but in 1840, when Wellington was founded as a Colony under the British Crown, it was a tiny settlement of huts ringed about by miles of untouched forests; and you realize with never-failing wonder how great a change has been wrought in a very short space of time. The town is built along the water front and up the hills behind, and is spreading every day higher up the hills and round the pleasant bays with which the rocky coast is indented.

To the stranger the noteworthy fact about these houses is the fact that they are of wood, and as nearly all have red roofs, when you see them perched upon the green hillsides, you wonder if you have come to some big toy town. Later you find that only the residential houses are invariably of wood; most of the public buildings—Post Office, banks, Town Hall and shipping offices—are of solid, grey concrete on steel frames; and both wood and steel are designed to resist the earthquake shocks which often visit the city, though not as a rule with great severity.

To a visitor from England all is strange and yet surprisingly the same as things left behind at home. Here is a big city with excellent shops, at which every imaginable need can be satisfied. You can buy clothes of every description—pretty dresses and hats or useful boots; there are jewellers and photographers; sellers of books, music or pianos; a depôt for Liberty's art needlework; and outside one of the florists' shops was a notice "Tree-ferns packed and despatched to all parts of the world."

Tramcars run through streets paved with wooden blocks. On all sides are men, women and children, dressed—many of them—in the latest fashions from London or Paris; and it is no foreign country that you have reached; for the shops have English names and familiar advertisements of Bournville Chocolate or Pears' Soap, and all these people are your own fellow-countrymen.

More than that, they are all possible friends, as I found before I had been two hours in Wellington. I asked some question of a lady in one of the tramcars, and after a little conversation she took me to a restaurant for "morning tea." Here, in a large and airy room, where all the small tables were decorated with vases of flowers on spotless white tablecloths, we were served with date-scones and sandwiches by girls tastefully dressed in green and white. The same day, my friend of the morning entertained me in her own home with afternoon tea and dinner. All this kindness was shown me because I was, as she explained, "a visitor from Home," and it was a pleasure to make me welcome in the new country. All through New Zealand I met with the same open-hearted friendliness and hospitality.

The shops, like those in other colonial towns, differ from English ones in having outside verandahs—roofs of corrugated iron on iron posts; the verandahs make the shop interior a little dark, but afford most useful screens either from sun or rain. The town is known as "Windy Wellington"; and it is said that you can anywhere recognize a Wellington man by the way in which he holds on his hat at street corners; the wind blows away microbes and keeps the inhabitants healthy, but is very wearing both to clothes and temper, and it is never wise to allude to it.

Neither is a strong wind always blowing. I have been in Wellington on calm days of glorious, sunny weather, when the town lay bathed in golden light, the blue harbour reflected the blue sky, and all the surrounding hills were blue, with peaks behind paling to grey in the distance. From the top of any of the hills that crowd closely together in narrow ridges behind Wellington, you look down on the town and on the irregular promontory on which it stands. On one side of the promontory is the harbour—a thread of blue water running out to the open ocean; and on a clear day, you look beyond the harbour to the coast of South Island with the snowy peaks of mountains near the coast. On the western side of the promontory, you can see over the thirty-three miles of Cook Strait to the nearest point of South Island, where blue headland and island, separated by purple shadows, rise confusedly from the sea.

At your feet, sheep feed on the short, sweet grass; and here and there in the gullies are still trees and ferns, reminders of days gone by.

The Dominion Parliament meets at Wellington in a wooden building that was until recently Government House; and the House of Representatives sits in the old ballroom, to which visitors are admitted by ticket. I went twice to hear the debate.

The Speaker's Chair is a small throne cushioned in crimson velvet, set under a carved canopy of polished brown wood; on the right sat Mr. Massey and the members of the Government; on the left, Sir Joseph Ward and the Opposition. There are galleries at either end, one for reporters, the other for strangers and members of the Upper House; and round the room was set a row of chairs for members' wives. The Mace was on a table in front of the Speaker's Chair.

The whole building is far too small, and will soon be replaced by a larger and grander house, of which the foundations have already been laid close to the present one.

Near the Houses of Parliament is the Museum, a small wooden building, in which there is very little room adequately to display all the treasures, and some have to be packed away and not shown at all.

The chief treasure is a Maori house—not a house for living in, but one in which the Maoris used to hold councils—a native Town Hall. It is a long, narrow house of one room, with a high-pitched, sloping roof, and it had originally one door and one window, both side by side at one of the narrow ends. Ranged against the two long walls are grotesque, carved, wooden figures of ancestors of the tribe of Maoris by whom the house was made—these figures are carved out of blocks of dull, red wood, and are three to four feet high; pieces of glittering blue and green shell are fastened in for eyes, and all the figures are ornamented very effectively with circular patterns in chip carving; there are sixteen figures on either side, and other figures again at both ends. The wall space between each figure should be filled in with reeds set close together, and crossed by narrow strips of wood fastened by thin bands of flax; in this house at Wellington, the reeds have all been replaced by wood, fluted, and painted a pale yellow; the ancestral figures too have been raised some way above the floor. Originally the walls were only the same height as the figures, and the roof sloped from the ridge-pole to the carved heads. The Maoris used to squat on the ground at their assemblies, so they did not need great height in their council halls.

Besides the entire Maori house, this museum has other specimens of Maori carving; such as a wooden verandah; and, set up on a high post, a tiny wooden room, slightly ornamented with carving; this latter the Maoris used as a food-store. Here too, I saw Maori clothing: aprons for men and women, all made of flax, woven tightly at the top and the ends left long and loose; there were long cloaks of flax, decorated with thrums of flax tied at intervals over the outer surface; sleeping mats too, neatly woven of flax.

Among the natural history exhibits the greatest curiosity is the "moa," an extinct New Zealand bird, who had no wings, but used to stalk over the country on enormous legs. No complete specimen of this bird has ever been found, but many eggs have been dug up, and sufficient bones and feathers for naturalists to reconstruct a life-sized model. There the bird stands, like a huge grey emu; as I stood by the side of it, my head reached the middle of the bird's thigh. There are several eggs on view—large white eggs, the size of cocoanuts; and some feathers, soft grey fluffy ones, like those of the emu, with whose feathers the model is covered. Present-day New Zealand birds are to be seen, with fish and beautiful shells from the South Seas. There are a few unexpected curios; such as a scrap of red and gold brocade from a cloak worn by Charles I; also certificates from Langley, Buckinghamshire, stating that two people named Powell, were in 1690 "buried in woollen, according to law."

Wellington has pretty public gardens, extending over many acres up the hillside and down to a well-wooded ravine, and everywhere native trees and ferns flourish. Below the hill is a broad stretch of level ground, where you find flower-beds gaily planted with English asters, zinnias and sweet peas, and shady pergolas with climbing roses.

There are Zoological Gardens too, spread over another hill on the opposite side of the town: the cages for birds and animals are set among trees—high dark pines, with undergrowth of lighter green—and the animals are rather hard to find as you trudge up and down the steep paths. A brown bear was in a cage, with the usual pole for him to climb: there were a fine African lion and lioness, sea-lions in a pond, monkeys, lemurs, squirrels and opossums; a good selection of many-coloured parrots and cockatoos from Australia, and most gawdy macaws from Malay.

I was most interested in a native "kiwi," which I persuaded the head-keeper to find for me. The kiwi lives in the bush and only walks abroad by night, so that when he is in captivity he retires during the day to the darkest, innermost recesses of his cage. The keeper found him and pulled him along by his beak—a bird the size of a large hen but on longer legs; it has a very long slender beak, and fluffy, grey feathers, and resembles its giant relation, the extinct moa, in having no wings.

In addition to gardens close to the town, Wellington has lately acquired several thousand acres of forest land round a sandy bay across the harbour. Here you find tall "rimus" and "totaras," green ferns and mosses, and many lovely tree-ferns—the variety with white undersides to their fronds, which in old days the Maoris used, like children in a fairytale, to mark out trails.

In springtime, the hills behind the town and the high cliffs along the shore are dazzling with golden broom and gorse; and on sandhills, where it has been planted to bind the sand, the yellow tree-lupin grows as freely as a buttercup.

Wellington has a large boys' school and fine University buildings. The University is affiliated to the Colleges of the other large towns, and women are admitted to degrees on equal terms with men.

There is always a steady air of bustle and business about Wellington; it is an important port—big ships come and go, with cargoes to be discharged and taken; and the fact that it is the seat of the Government makes it a necessity for the Governor and his suite to live here for several months of the year, and also brings New Zealanders from all parts of the Dominion.

CHAPTER II

STEWART ISLAND

Stewart Island lies south of the two main islands of New Zealand, separated by Foveaux Strait, a channel only thirty miles wide; but usually the sea there is rough, and the passage from South Island to Stewart Island in a small steam tug an unpleasant one. Stewart Island is about forty miles long from north to south, and has a coastline of between five and six hundred miles. In addition to Stewart Island proper there are numerous small islands, named and unnamed, scattered round the coast and away still further south. Stewart Island has two mountains, one two thousand, the other three thousand feet. The whole island is more or less hilly, and almost entirely covered with native bush.

There is one township called Oban, and a number of houses and cottages scattered about throughout the island. The steamer leaves the Bluff, the port of Invercargill, twice a week for Stewart Island, and takes passengers and mails to Oban's tiny wharf on Half-Moon Bay. There are several "accommodation houses" for tourists in Oban, all packed with people during the holiday season. The one in which I stayed soon after Christmas was so full that some of the visitors had to be housed in a small cottage in the garden, others in a canvas tent, and one in a bathroom. There were over forty visitors, and the one small drawing-room was so crowded that we were glad to pack ourselves carefully on a cushioned seat running all round the room.

The weather is very often wet on Stewart Island: it rained every day during the eight days I spent there, and though I walked out in all weathers, it was a pity to see the island so frequently through torrents of rain.

The usual plan for visitors is to make up a party of twenty or thirty from one of the hotels, hire a boat, take lunch, and boil the billy in one of the charming bays which abound all round the island. The day after I arrived was bright and sunny, just the day for such an expedition, and a large party of us started gaily in a motor sailing-cutter on a trip to Glory Bay and Ulva Island. The sea was calm, with sufficient wind blowing for us to dispense with the motor engine and trust only to the sails — a much pleasanter way of travelling than by motor. We had a delightful two hours' run to Glory Bay, where we anchored, and were all landed in a small rowing boat on a beach covered thickly with grey pebbles, large and small. Here we found a convenient fireplace fixed up — two iron supports firmly fastened in piles of stones, a stout branch of a tree laid across the uprights, and on the branch iron hooks dangling — all provided by Government, to prevent any danger of damage to the bush by careless picnic parties. On the hooks three billies were hung, a fire of sticks was lighted underneath, and when the water boiled, tea was sprinkled into each billy. In a few minutes the tea was ready, and we had cups of it ladled out to us with an enamelled mug, and sat down on the beach to an excellent picnic lunch of meat sandwiches, jam sandwiches, and tea. The trees and ferns came right down to the beach, and we looked across the quiet bay through a framework of greenery to a wooded island with the open sea beyond.

To-day I made acquaintance for the first time with the New Zealand "rata," one of the finest of the forest trees, attaining a height of fifty to a hundred feet. The rata is a species of myrtle, and was covered just now with crimson myrtle flowers, which in the sunlight turned a vivid scarlet, so that in patches the bush seemed to be on fire.

After lunch we explored the bay in the rowing boat, took snapshots, then again boarded the cutter, and sailed away for Ulva Island. This is an island several miles in extent, densely covered with bush; we landed, and walked for two miles along a very narrow, mossy track. The bush is very thick here, and shady: tall trees with ferns and mosses grow everywhere, while on the ground and over the tree-trunks and among the green moss are little fragile, white flowers. Even more noticeable than the trees are the tree-ferns—hundreds of them—with drooping, feathery green fronds crowning the slender, brown stems, which vary in height from six feet to forty. They grow in remarkable perfection and abundance on Stewart Island itself and on the islets round.

Our bush-track ended on a sandy beach. We then walked along a well-made path for a short quarter of a mile to a post office and store, kept by a solitary man who is the only inhabitant of the island, and who apparently lives there very contentedly; he collects the letters from the settlers on the neighbouring islands, and sells grocery, thread, stationery and other useful articles. We had been told that this was the most southerly post office in the world, but learnt later that in the Auckland Islands there is one many miles nearer the South Pole. Before we returned to the boat it began to rain, and rained steadily all the way back to Oban—real rain, which came down in sheets, and made it impossible to see anything of the scenery.

This expedition was the only one during my stay on Stewart Island, for after that, the sea was too rough for the boats to venture out. So stormy was it that twice within the week the steamer from the Bluff could not cross, and as the cable was not in working order, we were completely isolated.

A great part of Stewart Island belongs to the Government of New Zealand, and the bush is carefully protected, and heavy fines are imposed on anyone who wilfully damages it by fire or in any other way. For the benefit of tourists Government has spent some hundreds of pounds on making tracks in all parts of the island: in places simply a roughly beaten path, in others a "corduroy" track, formed of stems of tree-ferns laid side by side. The walks along these tracks are enchanting, either through dense bush, or skirting the edge of the forest, with charming views through green ferns and crimson rata to islands near and far, and the ever-distant ocean. Often the tracks lead down to some sheltered bay with steep tree-clad cliffs, whose bases are washed continually by the blue Pacific. Above one of these beaches stands the most southerly cable station in the world—an upright post, boarded four-square, through which the overland wire vanishes, to re-appear at the opposite station on the Bluff.

A SANDY COVE—STEWART ISLAND.

There are a number of native birds on Stewart Island. Chief among these are the "bell-bird" and the "tui." The bell-bird has a clear, musical call of its own, and can also imitate other birds. The "tui," is often called the "parson-bird," on account of two pretty white feathers which hang down under his chin like old-fashioned Geneva bands; the rest of his plumage is a dark glossy green; he is about the size of an English rook, bigger than the bell-bird, and like the bell-bird, sings well and musically. There are plenty of little birds; the robin, whose breast is yellow instead of red; tits, wax-eyes, wrens, and others, who dress in sober colours, and chirp to one another in pleasant, quiet notes. Round the coast you see penguins perched on the rocks. The smaller islands are favourite breeding-places for mutton-birds — grey birds about as big as quails — which are much esteemed by the Maoris as a delicacy: they are caught by the Maoris in quantities before the birds can fly, and after they have been plucked and smoked, they are preserved for future use in bags made of long ribbon seaweed.

Very good fish are to be caught near Stewart Island, as indeed all round the New Zealand coasts; blue cod is one of the most delicate, eaten either fresh or smoked, and the Stewart Island oyster-beds are famous from one end of the Dominion to the other.

The people who live on Stewart Island have the reputation of being rather lazy. Most of them are English, some of them are Maori half-castes. Part of the land has been cleared and is used for sheep runs, while some of the inhabitants are employed in cutting down timber. The chief business of the place is looking after the tourists who go in hundreds during the holiday months, and have a splendid holiday with boating, fishing, bathing and picnicing, or simply enjoying the mild climate and the lovely scenery.

Oban itself is a small township with a post-office; two small stores, where you can buy post-cards, caps, boots, pencils or grocery; and a baker's shop, with a baker who takes great pride in his home-made bread, and had never heard of German yeast. Of public houses there are none, as Stewart Island favours local prohibition, and no intoxicating liquors may be sold. There is an "Athenaeum" or reading-room, an Anglican Church, a Presbyterian Church, and some small meeting-houses for religious purposes.

The Athenaeum is used as a public hall for dances and concerts. One night a large party of us went to a concert there and heard songs and recitations. The chief item on the programme was the "haka," or ancient Maori war dance, which was performed by four half-caste Maori youths. There was no gliding movement, but much stamping of feet, gesticulating and shouting, all in unison: it is a most exhausting dance, and though it was most heartily encored, very little of the performance was given a second time.

As the weather was so bad, we were very much thrown on our own resources for amusement inside the boarding-house. Some sang or recited, or played on piano or violin, and one of the men proved a most dexterous and amusing conjurer. One night about fifty visitors joined in progressive euchre — a game which is much played in New Zealand, and another night we had a games party.

All through we contrived to be merry, in spite of the rain.

CHAPTER III
OVERLAND TO MILFORD SOUND

The walk along the Milford Track from Lake Te Anau to Milford Sound has been described by a New Zealand writer as "the finest walk in the world." It is a walk of thirty-three miles, through scenery of ever-changing variety and beauty, and is now undertaken annually by hundreds of tourists during the summer months.

Milford Track is in the South Island, among the lakes and fiords of Otago, and goes through an uninhabited and unexplored country of dense forest and inaccessible mountain. Tourists go by train to Lumsden, a small lowland township, and then on by motor coaches. These run for forty miles on a rough and stony road, almost impassable after heavy rain by reason of the mud and swollen creeks. At first it is rather an uninteresting drive, with flat "tussock" country on either side, and in the distance low hills; but gradually the scenery becomes wilder, the low hills give place to mountains bearing patches of never-melting snow, and the great lakes behind which they rise are surrounded by miles of untouched forest. The road here dwindles to vague ruts leading through the foothills of the more distant mountains, and tourists are taken for another twelve miles in wagonettes drawn by horses, to an accommodation house beside Lake Te Anau, where they spend the night.

Next day comes a further journey of thirty-three miles on a small steamer to the other end of the lake, and here in a little forest clearing is another solitary house and Post Office—Glade House—the starting-point for the walk.

I had gone with a friend, and we found eleven others all anxious to walk to Milford Sound, so we were a party of thirteen—five women and eight men—one happy family for the time being, all intent on enjoying everything as it came. Whatever luggage we took had to be carried on our backs, so we packed as few things as possible in stout canvas "swags" provided by Government for intending pedestrians, were rowed across a river in high flood, and plunged at once into the heart of the bush.

It was a delightful sunny day in midsummer. Before we began our walk there had been five days of incessant rain—every leaf dripped with moisture, and all about us was the noise of hurrying waterfall or river. The Clinton River, whose course we followed, was a wide torrent, rushing angrily over great boulders, or pausing for a while in deep quiet pools of clear green water. Numberless small streams flow from the mountains to join the Clinton, and many of them cross the track; sometimes they are bridged by a moss-grown, slippery tree-trunk; in other places they turn the track itself into a stream. There is no way round these creeks — you must simply wade through them; for my own part I did not wade through many, as one of the men of our party carried me on his back over all the worst of them. After the first two miles, this same kind friend insisted on taking my swag as well as his own, and I found that though I invariably began the day's tramp with swag on my back, I was not often allowed to carry it far.

CLINTON RIVER — TE ANAU LAKE.

The track is a narrow path, and green with the daintiest mosses, lovely to see and soft to tread upon. In places there is a good deal of native grass, and not infrequently grass from England too—cocksfoot or Yorkshire fog—and fallen beech leaves make a pleasant rustle as your feet brush through them. I had seen New Zealand bush in Stewart Island, and very pretty it is, but it cannot compare in grandeur or variety with the forests of Otago.

In New Zealand, the plants are still to be seen in the societies in which they have naturally grouped themselves through many generations of plant life—one group of plants in the river valleys, other groups by the sea coast or on Alpine heights; and wherever you go, you find fresh trees, ferns or mosses to admire, and always there is yet a chance of finding a plant that no one has seen before.

For several miles of the Milford track the prevailing tree is the black beech, one of the handsomest of the forest trees, with tall dark trunk and head of spreading branches, crowded with tiny, glossy, green leaves. Below the beeches grow other trees, at first somewhat thinly, but crowding more closely together the more deeply we penetrate into the forest. Among the trees are elegant tree-ferns in colonies of a hundred or more; through trees and fern-fronds gleams the sunlight; and beyond the overarching branches you catch fascinating glimpses of high mountains, their rugged summits sharply outlined against bright blue sky. Only the summits of the mountains for a few hundred feet are bare; steeply as they rise, in fact almost perpendicularly from the valley, they are yet clothed with trees in all shades of green, relieved here and there by great patches of rata blossom—the "red glory of the gorges"—and it is a constant wonder how the trees contrive to cling at all, much more how they can grow and flourish in such difficult circumstances.

Close to the track are fuchsias, which in New Zealand develop into big trees, and have pink ever-peeling bark, leathery grey-green leaves and flowers of dull purple. By the fuchsias grow veronicas, as tall as the fuchsias, now, at the end of January, in the full beauty of their abundant flower spikes, white or mauve; and with these are many trees of the compositæ family—olearias or senecios—all bearing bunches of white daisy-flowers. Many trees of the forest undergrowth have inconspicuous green or whitish flowers, and many-shaped leaves of glossy green—such are the broadleaf and the so-called fig and holly, growing side by side with the lancewood, whose leaves are saw-edged, grey-green swords. Everywhere too you find creepers and lianes—the tough black stems of the "supple-jack," and the trailing brambles of the "bush lawyer." The lawyer is a creeper which has hooked thorns on every little stem and leaf, and attaches itself relentlessly either to hair or clothes, like a dishonest solicitor, from whose clutches escape is difficult.

After a ten-mile walk we reached our stopping-place for the night—Pompolona Huts—two huts of corrugated iron, boarded throughout on the inside. One is for the men to sleep in; the other is divided into three rooms—ladies' bunk-room, dining-room and pantry. The dining-room is also the kitchen, and has a huge open fireplace and a "colonial oven" for baking bread, and over the fire is fixed an iron bar from which dangle hooks and pots. The food provided for us was the tinned meat and fruit usual in all camp life in New Zealand, with the addition of potatoes and hot boiled pudding.

The following morning we left Pompolona for McKinnon's Pass—the hardest bit of walking along the track. In fine weather the walk to Milford is easy enough, but going over the pass you are always liable to get caught in a blinding blizzard. Even in the valleys there is sometimes danger: a river or creek may rise several feet in a few hours, an insecure bridge may be loosened and washed away, or an unbridged stream suddenly become too high to ford.

After leaving Pompolona Huts, the path goes through country less thickly wooded, with occasionally wide open spaces, and little tarns of placid brown water. The ribbon-wood was in perfection in these open glades, bearing great trusses of delicate white flowers with a faint sweet perfume; they reminded us of cherry blossom, though the petals are more fragile, and the ribbon-wood actually belongs to the mallow family. The bark of the ribbon-wood is stripped off by the Maoris, and an inner layer, which looks like fine white lacework, is used in strips for making ornamental baskets. Little native flowers grow in the open: pale-mauve campanulas; tiny white daisies, and small yellow buttercups; a small, white cranesbill; and other little white things; and high in the sunlight stand masses of hardy, wiry bracken. Soon we are back in the forest, climbing gradually upwards under the trees. Throughout this walk one is continually amazed by the absence of bare, brown tree-stems; nearly every tree is covered all over with moss; trunks and branches fairly drip with it, as frost-laden trees do with icicles—moss of extraordinary beauty; some of it hanging in slender, swaying sprays, over a foot long; some short, with thick stems and feathery tufts—all of it in varying shades of green or brown. Among the mosses nestle fungi in strange diversity of shape and colour—white, pink, green or orange. Ferns, too, adorn the tree trunks, and often pale-green lichens, which from a short distance look like bunches of palest flowers.

There is a curious scarcity of birds. Stoats and weasels brought over from England and introduced into the bush in the hope that they would kill some of the superfluous English rabbits, have destroyed many native birds and their eggs, and it is now impossible to get rid of the stoats and weasels. The rare "kiwi" the wingless relation of the extinct "moa," lives still in these forests and is sometimes seen at night; I only saw it alive in the Wellington Zoological Gardens. We saw a number of "wekas"—Maori hens—brown birds about the size of a small pheasant, with very short tails and only rudimentary wings; they are not able to fly, but they walk very quickly through the fern. They had no fear of us, but walked across the path in front of us, or stood watching in the shade, and at night they prowled round the huts, looking for scraps and making weird calls to one another. We saw a few pigeons fluttering among the tree-tops, and some tits and tiny native wrens hopping from branch to branch; and by Te Anau were brown fantails, native cuckoos and a few small green-and-yellow parrakeets; and sometimes we heard the bell-bird's musical note, or the night owl hooting "more pork." English birds are now to be found in most parts of New Zealand—skylarks, sparrows, thrushes, blackbirds, starlings and goldfinches. I saw none of them on the way to Milford.

Butterflies are rare, though we did see a fair number of native ones, with dainty many-coloured wings, mottled in red, brown or yellow; and the lack of bird notes was in some degree made up for by the lively chirping of a black-and-yellow cricket. Very few insects were to be seen as we walked, but whenever we stopped, sandflies, tiny black flies whose bite is as bad as a mosquito's, came swarming round—eager for our blood.

Our only other enemies were the "biddabids"—the New Zealand substitute for an English burr. They are low-growing plants, the flower stalk a few inches high, and each flower stalk produces a dense brown head of seed, each little seed vessel furnished with four fine hooked claws. After brushing carelessly against a patch of these plants, stockings, skirt or jersey are found embroidered thickly with "biddies," and very difficult it is to rid oneself of them.

Towards the top of McKinnon's Pass, the mossy path becomes a stony track, winding on and up among Alpine flowers—white gentians and ourisias growing side by side with tall white or yellow mountain daisies. Then the track leads through brown tufts of snow grass, while almost at the summit you again find tarns of quiet brown water, in whose depths snowy mountains are reflected.

Here we breathed invigorating mountain air, and had a clear view of the mountains which before we had only partially seen through a fretwork of green. The top of the pass is more than three thousand feet above sea level—a narrow, rocky saddle blocking the head of the Clinton Cañon, and on the opposite side giving access to the valley of the Arthur River. Around the saddle are rugged peaks, rising to a height of five to seven thousand feet; some bare, others piled thickly with snow: and as we watched, avalanches came thundering down from one of the glaciers into the valley beneath. We could see the whole of the Clinton Cañon up which we had walked—a narrow valley, only half a mile wide, shut in by precipitous walls of four to seven thousand feet. Their rugged summits were all rock and snow; below they were clothed with dense forests reaching down to the valley, where the river wound in and out among the dark trees like a thread of light green ribbon.

Looking down the Arthur valley, which is much wider than the Clinton, we again looked over miles of forest backed by other rocky heights.

Below the pass, nine miles from Pompolona, are the Quinton Huts, our next resting place.

Near these are the Sutherland Falls, said to be the highest waterfall in the world, falling in three gigantic leaps from a height of nearly two thousand feet. They come roaring down over the steep hillside—a mighty volume of water ever thundering on brown rock fringed with luxuriant forest growth, and scattering showers of spray over the trees and over the grassy knoll on which you stand to watch them. They were only discovered in 1880, by a man named Sutherland, a settler from Scotland in the early days, who had a fancy for exploring.

At Quinton's we met another large party on their way back, and that night the huts were overcrowded: we were eleven ladies, with only nine bunks, so two slept in the dining-room. Next morning we all contrived to dress in perfect good temper; no one dreamed of making a trouble about anything, and it might have been excusable, as there was comfortable floor space for two, not for eleven; we had one small washstand, a small, square mirror hung on the wall for our only looking-glass, and a bench to serve as table and chair.

There is no telephone in working order beyond Pompolona Huts, and the arrival of so many visitors at Quinton's was unexpected.

The flour stored there had become damp, and could not be used in a hurry for baking by the men in charge, so at breakfast we ran short of bread: the ladies had as much as they wanted, but the men made up with biscuits and ginger nuts, and said sweetly that they liked them for a change.

The last day's stage is a walk of fourteen miles, on through the forest, beside the green Arthur river, and for five miles of the way skirting the edge of a lovely lake.

The river is twice crossed by long bridges: one a suspension bridge made of three flat planks, with strands of wire for protection on both sides; the other of "corduroy" planking—the planks all unhewn logs—supported in midstream on an enormous boulder.

The forest scenery grows greener and the ferns and mosses more abundant as you draw nearer the coast. Giant pines replace the beech trees. You now see thick clumps of mositure-loving "crape" ferns, whose long transparent fronds curl over at their tips like the heraldic Prince of Wales's feathers. The track is edged by frail bracken of palest green; ferns like filmy green lace drape the trees. Of such marvellous luxuriance is all the forest growth that trees and creepers and perching plants are inextricably interwoven, and often you cannot tell to which stem or trunk any branch belongs.

Ever since we left Glade House we had seen waterfalls, large and small, hundreds of them pouring down the mountains, culminating in the magnificent Sutherland Falls. Still as we walked we saw more waterfalls, none so high as the Sutherland Falls, but many exceedingly beautiful—some mere glittering threads of feathery white; others, which fell close beside the track, were falls both wide and high, crashing through the trees and breaking into seething white foam on huge grey boulders, resting at last in deep, green pools.

That day we had lunch in a tumble-down hut, where we found tea, a fireplace and enamelled tin mugs. We boiled the billy on the fireplace and then drank our tea out of the mugs, which one of the men thoughtfully rinsed in a lake close at hand: they were not clean, but nectar in golden goblets could not have tasted more delicious.

At the end of the track there is yet another hut, and usually a man in charge of it, who summons a motor launch from the head of Milford Sound, by letting off a charge of dynamite.

We met this man on the track taking a lady to Quinton Huts, and received full instructions as to where a small rowing-boat was to be found: so some of the party went on ahead, found the boat, and rowed across the sound to summon Mr. Sutherland and his launch, while the rest of us had afternoon tea and a rest.

The launch came and conveyed us safely to our journey's end—a lonely accommodation house with a Post Office, at the edge of forest and ocean. The house is a one-storied building of wood, with corrugated iron roof and a verandah: there is a garden, with vegetables, currants and raspberries. Grass grows right up to the house. Sheep feed on the grass, and stroll even into the bathroom, which has a door without a lock. The house is comfortably furnished, and considering its distance from anywhere, surprisingly well supplied with food and other necessaries. It is even possible to buy shoes here.

The following morning we chartered the launch and were taken down the Sound and out on the Pacific Ocean.

Milford Sound is ten miles long. At its narrowest it is only a quarter of a mile wide, but where it joins the ocean about two miles. The whole sound is a deep narrow channel, formed originally by glacial action. Mountains rise straight out of the water, covered thickly with bush for some four thousand feet, until the trees stop abruptly on reaching the line of winter snow: you here see a wonderful contrast—green leaf and crimson rata-flower on the brown rock.

Here again are waterfalls. One falls sheer in a narrow unbroken column for five hundred feet; another falls in two great leaps; the higher of the two leaps curves far out from the rock and was turned by the sunshine into a golden halo.

On one side of the Sound is Mitre Peak, over five thousand feet, with bare pointed summit: opposite stands the Lion, his massive rounded crest slanting down to a narrow ridge among the forest; and behind the Lion, far away, beyond a narrow tree-girt cove, is a yet higher peak, snow-laden above the green. As we sailed out to sea, we saw black cormorants watching for their prey; gulls—white with brown bars on their wings—came flying round the boat; and, scrambling out of the water and up the rocks at the side in most ungainly fashion, were small and terrified black-and-white penguins.

In winter time, when for many miles the overland track lies buried in snow, a small steamer plies up the Sound once a month with provisions and letters for the inhabitants of the one lonely house, and sometimes a Government boat goes to Milford and other Sounds to visit lighthouses and a few scattered settlers.

There is said to be one old man who lives quite alone in a hut on one of the West Coast Sounds, and to whom the Government steamer regularly takes his old age pension changed into food and clothing; the Captain always gives orders to the men who take food for "Maori Bill" to go provided with a spade and a Prayer Book as well, in case the poor old man should be dead.

We could only spend two nights at Milford before beginning the walk back to Glade House, which we reached two days later, one happy family, as we had set out.

LAKE WAKATIPU.

CHAPTER IV

THE COLD LAKES OF OTAGO

One of the favourite holiday excursions in the South Island is to the Cold Lakes of Otago.

In England it is hardly necessary to explain that lakes are cold, but in New Zealand you never know—you find a pool of hot sulphur water under the Southern Alps, and hot creeks and lakes in the thermal district of North Island.

The largest of the Otago lakes is Wakatipu—a lake like a beautiful blue serpent. It is fifty miles long and varies in width from one mile to three and a half, as it winds in and out among stately mountains. Situated on one of the curves is Queenstown, a regal little city by the great lake, happily remote from the world and its bustle. It has no railway, and you reach it either by motor car, or more often by steamer—a delightful trip of twenty-five miles from the southern end of the lake.

I meant to spend one week at Queenstown, but the place and its surroundings are so beautiful, and I met such a number of pleasant people there, that in the end I stayed for three weeks, and left with many regrets. There are several good hotels. The one at which I stayed was separated from the lake only by a broad road. From the windows of the hotel I looked out upon tall drooping willows, fringing the blue water; and sometimes at sunset saw a wonderful display of crimson and gold behind grim purple mountains towards the head of the lake. The lake is stocked with trout; enormous specimens came right up to the landing stage to be fed; these particular fish are pets of the town and may on no account be killed.

From Queenstown tourists are driven to the Skipper's Gorge. It is a drive of sixteen miles through a strange country of bleak and rugged hills, which are bare of all vegetation but scanty, coarse grass and occasional low-growing shrubs; and on the hillsides gaunt grey rocks stand up, like pillars or ruined castles. Sheep can find pasturage on the hills, and as you drive up, you see in the valleys scattered homesteads on the stations, or the school of some tiny township. The district is thinly populated now, but in the sixties and the days of the Otago gold-rush, mines abounded in every little river-bed: a fair amount of gold is still found by sluicing and dredging.

Life is lonely and hard in these far back places, either on station or gold-claim; and sometimes you hear sad tales of men and women, whom the loneliness drives to drink or suicide.

The Skipper's Drive is a marvel of engineering. The road is cut out of the sides of the hills and the narrow thread winds round them, with often on the one hand a precipice over a hundred feet deep, and no protection beyond a low stone coping or a few inches of rough soil. The drivers are always skilful, and horses bred among the mountains can be trusted to keep their feet, so there is little need for alarm.

Some of these remote valleys have wide and deep rivers and not many bridges. When the river-bank is high on both sides, wire ropes are stretched across and a very simple wooden cage hung on the ropes, and anyone wishing to cross sits on the floor of the cage with his legs dangling over the river-bed and pulls himself to the opposite side. At the Skipper's Gorge we found a cage of this kind, and I was able to enjoy crossing a river in such an unusual way. On a calm day there is no difficulty, but it must be dangerous in a high wind.

The most delightful tracks round Queenstown are either for walking or riding. Whichever way you go—up one of the hills or along a track near Lake Wakatipu, you are always surrounded by wonderful scenery.

From the top of Ben Lomond, at a height of between five and six thousand feet, you look down upon the lake, in colour a bright blue, toning to purple at the sides; rising steeply from the water, and sloping away from it to bare jagged peaks are mountains of five and six thousand feet; while far away, encircling the lake-head, are yet higher peaks, and to east and north, piled one behind the other, peaks and ever more peaks, purple and grey or whitely crowned with snow.

Riding near the lake, you see everything more intimately. There are pines and weeping willows by road or track, gum-trees and poplars in garden and paddock; on the hillside are the tall, fresh, green fronds and the withered, brown ones of the bracken, making an undergrowth for elegant cabbage-trees, sturdy fuchsias and currants, and trailing bush lawyers. Below, in the still, blue water is an exact reflection of each outline of the purple hills above.

A steamer goes on certain days each week from Queenstown to the northern end of the lake. Beyond, after a twelve mile drive, you reach two hotels and some scattered sheep-runs, on the very edge of cultivation. Here are wide river-valleys and tiny lakes, towering mountains and snowy glaciers; and the hills are clothed with magnificent beech forests, through which few people have as yet attempted to penetrate.

I finally left Lake Wakatipu and Queenstown by motor coach. A drive of forty-eight miles took me to Lake Wanaka.

It was a sunny summer day, and all was gay; the hills were blue and the valleys green. As the car zig-zagged up the Crown Range, we looked down on the blue surface of Wakatipu shimmering in the sunlight, and on the windings of the Molyneux River twisting among the hills in ribbons of blue—a blue more vivid and intense than that of the shining sky overhead.

At Wanaka is a tiny township, named Pembroke. Here I stayed at a one-storied wooden hotel of many detached passages and cubicles, all standing in an old-fashioned English garden. This garden had wide herbaceous borders crowded with flowers; tall, drooping willows and excellent vegetables; and among the flower-beds were apple trees, and many plum trees laden with more ripe plums than the proprietor or his guests could possibly eat. There was even a giant mulberry tree, heavily laden with fruit.

From Pembroke, visitors go in an oil launch, capable of holding sixty passengers, on an excursion of forty miles up the lake and picnic at the head of it.

I do not think the reflections on Wanaka are quite so marvellous as on Wakatipu, but the lake as a whole is equally beautiful, and the general plan is the same in both—a long narrow lake among high mountain-peaks.

The mountains which surround Wakatipu are bare of any but small low-growing trees, and on that account you see and enjoy their outlines more perfectly; but on the other hand, the tall, dense forest-growth, which fills many of the mountain gullies and fringes the shore of Wanaka, gives to the landscape an added richness.

As at Wakatipu, the mountains which surround Wanaka are only the foreground for other and higher peaks, stretching ever to the west, purple or streaked with snow.

There are small islands in the lake. At one of these we disembarked, and climbed up a steep track among the scrub. At the top we found, nestling under a rocky crag, a charming lakelet of three acres, at a level of four hundred feet above the main lake. Round the irregular, rocky shore of the tiny lake grow trees—ratas and other smaller ones—leaning over the water; and in the lake are minute islands with little stunted trees—all as though planned by some Japanese artist You stand at the edge of the Japanese garden, and look through its fringing trees and out upon the big blue lake to steep, bare hills beyond.

Pembroke is a centre from which to go deerstalking. I saw no deer, but later in Christchurch I saw fine antlers which some sportsman had bagged.

Coaches and motor cars connect Pembroke with Clyde and the railway of Central Otago.

I chose to go by motor thinking it would be quicker, but alas! the road is rough, and the car broke down; and I had to be picked up by the horse coach, which obligingly ran on the same day.

Clyde is on the edge of the fruit-growing district. At the hotel, I soon made friends with an elderly gentleman who took me to see peaches and apricots growing as standards; and the owner of the trees let me pick as many peaches as I could eat—and very delicious they were!

Next day Clyde had a fruit and flower show in the town hall, and the farmers round all came to exhibit their produce and to see what others were doing. It was a little show, but held much promise of great things in the future.

The peaches were excellent and so were the plums and apples, there were very few apricots, but good, ripe figs and blackberries: the presence of any blackberries at all in the show was perplexing, as throughout New Zealand the English blackberry bramble has grown and spread far too vigorously, and is now considered a "noxious weed," which must be destroyed whenever possible. In the vegetable section were good clean tomatoes, pumpkins, potatoes, beans and carrots. For plants in pots the competition was slight, and a fuchsia and two small heliotropes all won prizes. There were two stiff bouquets and a few table decorations, and on a raised platform, freehand drawings from the primary schools, and several good specimens of embroidery and plain needlework.

The main purpose of the show was to encourage apple growing for export; different kinds were exhibited which are being tested for their flavour and keeping properties, and demonstrations were given in the best way of packing.

The soil round Clyde is white and sandy, and looks barren and hopeless, but I was told that it is really so rich in plant foods, that, given sufficient water, it will grow anything.

The railway from Clyde runs through a queer, wild country of rock and scattered stones; where the only vegetation consists in rare tufts of tussock grass and frequent dabs of pale green moss, which make you think the ground must be turning mouldy from lack of use. There is very little level ground and not much scope for a railroad: the train simply forces its way along, creeping through tunnels, and clinging hardily to the hillsides above steep precipices yawning below.

People do come now and then to meet the train at some wayside station, but there is little traffic in such a desolate land.

Later we ran through deep gorges, whose steep sides have patches of dark bush above the rushing Taieri River. The gorges widen out into the broad Taieri Plain, with its farms and woollen factory; and towards evening the train steamed into Dunedin's smart railway station.

CHAPTER V
THE NEW ZEALAND EDINBURGH

The town of Dunedin is Scotch in name and origin and in the number of its inhabitants who are of Scotch descent, and is renowned for the enterprise of its settlers and the solid worth of its buildings and institutions. It was founded, in 1848, by Scotch Presbyterians; and though there is now an Anglican Bishop of Dunedin, and Ministers of various denominations, Presbyterianism is yet the dominant form of Christianity. Like other New Zealand settlements, the new Scotch colony consisted in its early days of a few small huts at the edge of the forest. A part of one of these huts, made of "wattle and daub," has been preserved, and is to be seen in the "Early Settlers' Hall." Here, too, are portraits of the "old identities," and pictures of the small sailing vessels in which they crossed the ocean, and of Prince's Street, the one street of the embryo town. Such grim, determined faces those early settlers had, and it must have needed all their courage to face life in a strange land among possibly unfriendly natives, with no roads, an almost complete absence of eatable fruits or vegetables, no fresh meat except fish and birds; and in a country covered either with impenetrable forest or rough tussock grass. Now all round Dunedin the forests have been cleared, and the low hills, which rose on either side of Otago Harbour from the Heads to the town wharves, are sown with British grass, and the land is divided up into sheep runs and dairy farms.

Dunedin itself is a city set on a hill facing the harbour. Half-way up the hill, adding greatly to the health and beauty of the place, is the Town Belt—a broad band of native bush, left uncut between the business part of the town and residential suburbs, to keep for all time a forest way into the open country beyond. From some point above this belt of trees, you may look down upon the present city with the spires and towers of Churches, University and other fine buildings; upon the narrow harbour and the long neck of undulating hilly country, which on the south divides it from the open ocean. On the north are hills and valleys, with a sprinkling of houses and thick groves of trees; and as you walk or ride towards the west, you see a wide green plain stretching inland to distant hills; and immediately below, on the edge of the plain, rise the chimneys of the Mosgiel woollen factory, whose rugs are famous the world over.

Between Prince's Street and the harbour lay in the beginning some furlongs of uninhabitable swamp-land, soon reclaimed by the zeal of the early colonists. These intrepid settlers cut off the top of the small hill on which the chief Presbyterian Church now stands, and with the material thus obtained they filled in the marsh and procured a good foundation for many of their public buildings—railway station, Post Office, University, banks, and the offices of the shipping companies.

OTAGO HARBOUR.

The railway station is a very pretty one—the finest in the Dominion—of grey stone, with projecting turrets and tall slender clock-tower, faced with stone and red brick; the trains run into it by way of a dangerous level crossing over a wide street between town and harbour. The Post Office is, like others in colonial towns, a large building, with separate departments for everything: stamps in one room, money orders in another, private letter-boxes in another part, and here the telegraph and cable department is in a distinct block in another street; private letter-boxes are found in New Zealand even in small post offices, deliveries are not very frequent, and people often find it more convenient to fetch their own letters. A New Zealand post office is planned with scrupulous regard to efficiency, and is straightforward enough when you have learnt your way about it, but at first each fresh one is, like the different tramway systems, exceedingly puzzling.

Dunedin publishes three daily newspapers and three weekly ones—a fair number for a town of sixty thousand people—but in New Zealand all towns of any size publish one or more daily papers, and nearly every small country township has a local paper once or twice a week. The weekly papers here and in other large towns have capital illustrations and give news of the world and of New Zealand generally; the daily papers have the latest cables from London and all parts of the world, and for other news are chiefly concerned with the happenings in their own particular town and province; so that in Dunedin you hear very little of what is going on in Auckland.

Dunedin has large public gardens laid out with green lawns and many-coloured flower-beds; in the gardens are greenhouses too, with orchids, palms, high pink begonias and trailing red fuchsias; among groups of dark trees flows the Water of Leith, and on a shady lake swim black swans and Paradise ducks; the latter are native birds of particularly gay and attractive plumage.

In these gardens, as well as in all other public gardens in the Dominion, there is a bandstand where a band plays frequently, and here in the summer the citizens hold garden fêtes. I went with friends to one such fête on a sunny afternoon in March. It was held with the object of obtaining money for the further beautifying of the town by planting waste spaces with trees and flowers. Many hundreds of spectators stood round a large platform, erected for the display of the competitions; there were "poster" competitions for the children, gymnastic exhibitions by different schools, decorated bicycles and go-carts, and children danced with coloured ribbons round a maypole. On the lawns were putting and bowling contests for grownups. Tea was served in big tents, and all who could spent the afternoon either in helping or in being entertained.

Dunedin and Otago generally have the reputation of being the most friendly and hospitable parts of the Dominion: personally I found Dunedin people entirely kind; they took me on trust and made me welcome in the happiest way, and I felt as though I had known them all my life.

CHAPTER VI
AMONG THE SOUTHERN ALPS

My first experience of tourist travelling in New Zealand was a trip to the Southern Alps, with a stay among the mountains of only six days. It was a very short visit, but long enough for something of the fascination of the mountains to take hold of me and bring me back later for several months. From Christchurch the traveller sees, a hundred miles away, on the western side of the Canterbury Plain, the whole range of the Southern Alps, a wonderful rampart of snowy peaks; and it was with eager curiosity that I set out on the journey thither.

Not many years ago the mountains were almost inaccessible and it was necessary to ride the greater part of the way. Now a railway winds up among the southern foothills, and during seven months of the year an excellent service of motor cars runs regularly three days a week between Fairlie, the railroad terminus, and the mountain hostel, ninety-six miles further. Fairlie is a small township, with two hotels, Post Office, a bank and a few shops in its main street. Round about the township are grassy hills with many "cabbage trees," their bare brown stems surrounded by one or more tufts of narrow green streamers, which wave lightly in the breeze: the cabbage tree is a species of lily, and in the early summer has long panicles crowded with creamy white blossoms among the green leaves. It grows on hill, plain or swamp, and always on good soil.

Tourists spend the night at Fairlie, and start in the car next morning punctually at eight o'clock.

This district has all been taken up by settlers for farms and sheep runs. We drove past "paddocks," as all fields are called in New Zealand, white with English ox-eye daisies or dazzlingly yellow with great bushes of broom, and saw homesteads sheltered by clumps of oaks, poplars, willows or pines.

The road climbs steadily uphill to the top of Burke's Pass, more than two thousand feet above sea level, and for the rest of the way goes through "tussock" country, a land of hill and plain covered as far as eye could see with tufts of brown grass. On a rainy day such a landscape, stretching on interminably in one uniform tint of brown has a very desolate appearance, but when the sun shines the brown hills gleam yellow in the distance and develop beautiful purple shadows in their hollows, and big white clouds floating above them make purple shadows too: then, beyond the rounded hills stand blue mountains, rugged and mysterious, their summits streaked with snow. In the heart of the hills you come unexpectedly upon a lovely blue-green lake, six miles long, fed by glacier streams, a blue mountain torrent rushing out of it. Thirty miles further on we reached yet another lake— Lake Pukaki—twice the size of the first, and green rather than blue. Behind this lake, though still forty miles away, we saw Mount Cook, half hidden by clouds. Mount Cook, or as the Maoris called it, "Aorangi, the Sky Piercer," is 12,349 feet in height, the Monarch of the Southern Alps, and the loftiest mountain in New Zealand. The Maoris gave names to many of the high peaks in both islands, but knew them only from afar; they regarded them with reverent awe and had no wish to invade their solitudes. The honour of being the first to reach the summit of Mount Cook rests with three New Zealanders, who climbed it successfully on Christmas Day, 1894.

ROAD BETWEEN FAIRLIE AND THE HERMITAGE.

The tussock country is devoted to sheep runs, varying in size from one thousand to twenty thousand acres; the runs used to be as large as sixty thousand acres, but all the larger runs have now been split up by Government with a view to closer settlement. Merinos and crossbreds thrive very well, but as from three to five acres are needed to support one sheep, the runs need to be a fair size. Between the tufts of tussock grow some finer grasses, and English white clover and sorrel are gradually spreading; the tussock grass is often burnt in patches, so that the sheep may have the fresh shoots which spring up from its roots. Wire fences divide the runs, and at intervals are posted collie dogs, with a barrel for kennel, to keep a watchful eye on their masters' sheep; houses are very rare, ten miles or more apart, the older ones surrounded by flourishing trees.

The road is kept in repair by men who go about with carts and long shovels and collect stones from the bank or any convenient pit by the roadside. There are stones everywhere, large and small, carried down from the mountains in the far-away days when all the valleys were filled with enormous glaciers. The road-menders are paid nine shillings a day, wet or fine; in wet weather they do no work, but as they have no fixed homes and sleep where they can, it is not a life to be envied. Every few miles along the road are posts with hooks—generally old horseshoes—and on the hooks, as the car went by, the driver hung the mail bags, and as a rule, a man on horseback came trotting up to fetch them. The telephone wire runs close to the road the whole way, and the tourist cars are provided with spare wires, which can be attached in case of need.

On leaving Lake Pukaki, the road skirts the hillside above a valley some four miles wide, where on the right the Tasman River flows through a level swamp. In front, ever growing nearer, are the High Alps, range behind range, at first green or brown, then grey and purple, with glaciers gleaming whitely among the shadows.

Our destination, in December, 1912, was the Old Hermitage, and this we safely reached punctually at 5 p.m.

The Old Hermitage was a small hotel managed by the New Zealand Government Tourist Department. It was a comfortable, one-storied building, made of "cob"—a mixture of clay and grass—boarded inside, and with an outer casing made of corrugated iron. It was the first house built in New Zealand for the accommodation of climbers and has been a delight to many visitors; during the last few years it has proved far too small, and in 1912 a big hotel was being built on a better site, a mile away from the old one.

The old house stands in a hollow at the very foot of the mountains, with the verandah facing Sefton's snowy peak. On either side of it are other mountains cleft by deep gullies, and to the sides of gullies and mountains cling hardy Alpine shrubs, while above the vegetation come shingle slopes and naked brown rock, and higher still, at about 5,000 feet, the unmelting snow.

Most of the tourists who stop at the Hermitage for longer than one night wish to go for some excursion up one of the glaciers or mountains. The particular expedition that newcomers generally take is one to the Hooker Glacier with a night spent in an Alpine hut. At the Hermitage everything is provided by Government—

guides, horses, alpenstocks or ice-axes, puttees, and even climbing boots. The Government boots are well made and kept in many sizes for hire, but the more comfortable plan is to take strong boots and have nails put in them.

The head guide decided that I, like other "new chums," should go with a party of ladies to the Hooker, so off we set, carrying alpenstocks, and feeling very important; the head guide himself came with us, taking in his rucksack any clothes we needed as well as food. Our road lay up the valley, over ancient moraines covered with scanty tussock grass, low-growing brooms, heaths and dainty Alpine flowers. The New Zealand Alpine flowers are usually white—helichrysums, daisies or heaths; though sometimes the daisies are yellow, and there are mauve campanulas, and the white violets have streaks of mauve. To-day we saw, growing in profusion, clumps of yellow spear-grass, its leaves half an inch wide with points like needles, and bearing long spikes of dull yellow flowers—a plant known as "Spaniards" and very handsome, but best admired at a respectful distance.

All the centre of this valley is filled with ice many feet thick, piled high with boulders large and small, and powdered over everywhere with grey dust; the Mueller Glacier which comes down from Mount Sefton brings with it an amazing amount of débris, and its terminal face is hardly visible; all is a weird scene of unrelieved desolation—one vast rubbish heap—and only on looking very closely where a glint of white or green shows through the silt, can you feel assured that the foundation of it is ice and not solid rock. We crossed the Hooker River by two suspension bridges—wooden planks hung on chains, which sway alarmingly in the wind, while the torrent brawls noisily many feet below, and walked along a narrow track up the Hooker Valley.

Here we found ourselves among the Mount Cook lilies in full flower, by the river and up the hill sides, and at our feet in sheets of white among the stones—a perfect natural rock-garden. These so-called lilies are a species of ranunculus (Ranunculus Lyallii), they have smooth green stalks two feet high, and the flowers are in clusters, five to nine flowers on each stem, the individual flowers two inches across, pure white petals round bright yellow centres; the leaves stand below the flower heads, every leafstalk bearing a green cup—it is a large and perfect cup, and can be used to drink from, and after rain you find water waiting for the thirsty traveller. Other Alpine plants were here too—big white daisies with fleshy green leaves, yellow mountain celandines, many small-leaved native shrubs, and intruding patches of red English sorrel. Under a huge boulder, surrounded by lilies, we had our lunch of sandwiches and tea, and it was here that I first learnt the excellence of tea made in a "billy." The billy is a tin pail, large or small, and takes the place of both kettle and teapot, as when the water boils tea is sprinkled into it, the lid is left on for a few minutes and the tea is poured straight from the billy into the cups.

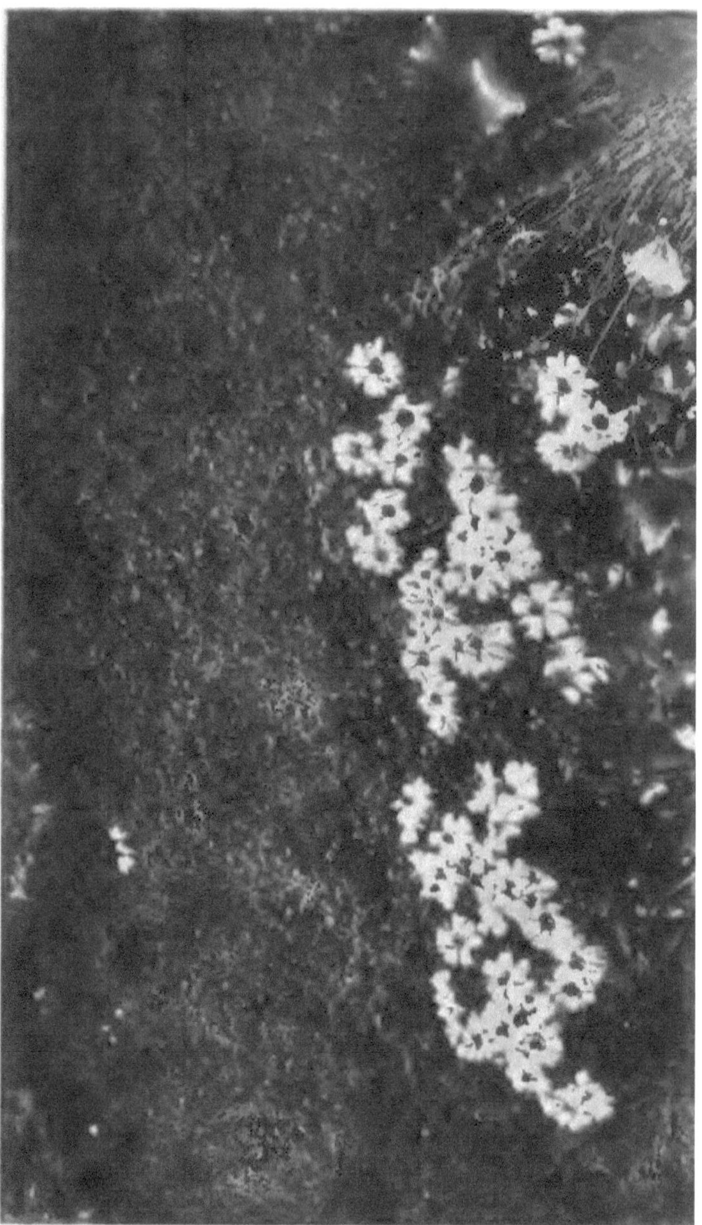

MOUNT COOK LILIES.

After a rough scramble among stones and over noisy streams hurrying to join
the glacier below, early in the afternoon we reached the Hooker Hut, set in a level
space against the mountain side. In front of the hut are the peaks of the Mount
Cook Range—bare brown rock below, but always snow on their summits. At the
foot of a steep cliff flows the Hooker Glacier, and at the head of the glacier towers

Mount Cook, a mighty, snow-clad giant. The hut itself is, like most of the New Zealand Alpine huts, a serviceable building of corrugated iron on a framework of wood, lined with thick linoleum. This one is divided into two rooms with six bunks in each; one room for the ladies' bedroom, and the other to serve as living room and men's bedroom. The living room has a table, two large chests, benches and a kerosene oil-stove.

The only living creatures we saw by the hut were the mountain parrots—"keas" as they are called in imitation of their cry which often resembles the word "ke-a" shrieked slowly and harshly; they have many calls and sometimes remind one of a whining puppy, sometimes of a crying baby, and on a wet day a kea will sit on a rock and croak until the dismal monotony of his cry compels you to speak severely and shy stones at him. They have black, curved parrot beaks and sage-green plumage, and when they fly, disclose pretty red backs, and a patch of red feathers on either wing. They are most friendly, inquisitive birds, and came up to the door of the hut and took the greatest interest in our doings.

Our guide gave us a good dinner of hot soup, cold mutton, boiled tomatoes, canned apricots and tea. Soon after dinner we turned in. The bunks have wooden sides with strong canvas nailed across. On the canvas is laid a soft down mattress, and with the addition of a pillow and many grey blankets you have a very comfortable bed. Keas seem to need very little sleep; they roosted on the roof of the hut, and apparently overbalanced when asleep and went slipping down the iron over our heads. Finally they gave it up, and began calling to one another long before it was light. The only other sounds were of occasional avalanches slipping down the mountain sides. We got up at 5 a.m., and by 7 o'clock started for the glacier, along a very rough track over the moraine, then across patches of dirty snow. At last we were on the glacier and walked over the snow a couple of miles towards Mount Cook, getting good distant views of mountains and glaciers. So early in the season the glacier is covered with last winter's snow, only here and there are there crevasses wide and deep enough to show the beautiful green ice tints. Our feet sank into the snow at every step; and after a luncheon of sardine sandwiches and iced pineapple, which we ate sitting on our alpenstocks in the middle of the glacier, we were glad to turn and regain the track.

When next I stayed at the Hermitage, fifteen months later, the new hotel had just been opened, and was crowded with tourists coming and going. The time was early autumn and the weather perfect, with cold nights and days of glorious sunshine, and I was able to see far more of the mountains than had been possible before.

On the river flats, except for white gentians and mauve or white campanulas, most of the flowers were over; but in their place glowed berries of red, yellow, white, blue or black; and near the snow line was the New Zealand edelweiss, with quaint grey flower and leaf. After the hot summer the glaciers were very much broken, with the surface snow melted and the ice foundation traversed by many crevasses of ten to a hundred feet; and walking on the narrow ice ridges between the crevasses needed a steady head and well nailed boots.

The largest glacier in New Zealand is the Tasman Glacier, which is eighteen miles long, and at its widest two and a half miles across. It flows parallel with the main Divide of the Alps, receiving several tributary glaciers in its course, until it ends abruptly in a high wall of stones and dirty grey ice, five miles from the Hermitage. To reach the head of the glacier is a two days' expedition. On the first day you ride for fourteen miles on horseback along a narrow track, which for part of the way is a mere scratch on the side of the mountain high above the glacier bed. After one night in a hut you then, if the weather is fine, go on the next day for a ten mile tramp over the solid ice.

Right at the head of the Tasman, on a little plateau two or three hundred feet above the glacier, has been built a narrow stone platform on which stands a tiny hut. It is almost on the snow line, and the only vegetation is the wiry snow grass and a few intrepid gentians and lilies, which find shelter against great boulders. No keas venture so high, only a stray gull had flown up from the river valleys.

Standing outside the hut I saw, under perfect conditions, one of the grandest mountain views to be found in New Zealand or any other country. Facing me was a mighty wall of mountains—all the highest peaks of the Southern Alps, giants of nine to twelve thousand feet, with snowy summits and great snowfields and buttresses of naked rock. On the extreme right, a dome of pure white snow, over nine thousand feet high; and, encircling its base, the beginning of the Tasman glacier, a great expanse of snow ever feeding the great ice river, whose course could be seen for twelve miles, sweeping majestically underneath the mountains, until, beyond Mount Cook, it was hidden by a spur of the range on which I stood. Mount Cook fitly dominated the scene, a thousand feet higher than any other mountain, with its summit a long toothed ridge of snow-clad peaks. I watched while the sun set and all the glacier lay in shadow: soon the snows of the lower slopes of the mountains became a cold, dead white, while their summits flushed with deep rose-colour against pure blue sky.

CHAPTER VII
CHRISTCHURCH

Christchurch ranks next to Auckland as the second largest city in the Dominion, and in its general plan and social atmosphere is the most English of New Zealand towns. It was founded in 1850 by members of the "Canterbury Association," with the Archbishop of Canterbury at their head, as a settlement in connection with the Church of England, and was named after Christchurch College, Oxford. The exclusive character of the colony was soon found to be impracticable—all colonists were made welcome, and at the present time, Christchurch is sometimes spoken of as the happy home of cranks.

When the first colonists, the "Canterbury Pilgrims," as they were called, reached New Zealand, they landed ten miles from the city of to-day, at a port which they named Lyttleton, and the first rough huts were built at the entrance to a long and sheltered harbour running inland between wooded hills. Lyttleton is still the port of Christchurch, and is connected with it by a railway tunnelling through the hills. Christchurch itself stands on the edge of the Canterbury Plain, with the Port Hills on the south, the ocean on the east, and unlimited space for growth on the north and west.

In the centre of the city is the Cathedral, a fine building of grey stone with a noticeable spire, standing in an open grassy square. Round this square are set shops, hotels and the Post Office. From the Cathedral Square many roads radiate, and electric trams run in all directions—out into the country, or down to the sea shore, five miles away. The streets are straight and at right angles, and bear the names of English Cathedral cities—Hereford, Gloucester, Durham or Salisbury—but High Street runs diagonally through the squares; and the river Avon, bridged by many picturesque bridges of stone or wood, winds through the town, preventing any possibility of crowding or primness.

All the streets are wide, and the river banks are green with grass and rushes. In the streets and along the riverside grow English oaks, sycamores, poplars or birches, and, more striking than all, hundreds of weeping willows which here grow to a great height, their supple branches drooping gracefully into the water. I have never seen English woodland trees so beautiful in an English autumn as the same trees are in Christchurch, where the leaves remain on the trees later than at Home, and each leaf turns a vivid yellow—a very pageant of gold in the clear bright sunlight under a cloudless sky.

RIVER AVON AT CHRISTCHURCH IN WINTER.

On one side of the town, the Avon flows through five hundred acres of parkland, part of which is highly cultivated and planted with flowers and trees from all parts of the world—a lovely garden with trim lawns and shady, gravelled paths. The greater part of the reserve is kept as a recreation ground for football, golf and tennis; and has also broad, tree-shaded avenues, down which you may canter on horseback, and see beyond the trees the blue rounded summits of the Port Hills, and many miles away to the west, the snowy peaks of the Southern Alps.

In addition to the Cathedral, Christchurch has many other churches and very fine public buildings. Most of them are built of grey stone, and all stand in prominent places, where they can easily be found and admired. The Supreme Court of Law is on a grassy knoll above the river; the Municipal Buildings and the Public Library among groups of trees on the riverside; and close to the public gardens are the Museum, the University buildings of Canterbury College, and another group of buildings known as Christ's College—a big school for boys, founded on the model of an English Public School.

Christchurch Museum, like the one at Wellington, has a fine Maori house with its series of carved ancestral figures; and here the walls are of reed left intact as the Maoris made them, and the house has on the outside a very ornamental display of painting in a bold freehand pattern, coloured red, white and blue. There are rare and beautiful examples of Maori cloaks; one of flax, with the feathers from pigeons' necks woven in closely, so that you see a rich blue and green feather garment; another was made of strips of dog-skin woven in with the flax; another had white dogs' tails, and yet another had feathers of the native kiwi, a soft grey, like those of the emu or the extinct moa. There are many curiosities from the islands of the Pacific; a large and fragile canoe made of thick reeds fastened together with reed thongs from the Chatham Islands; and from some island further north a most gruesome curio—a record of a cannibal feast—a log of wood bound with flax to a smaller piece, and between the two a neat bundle of human bones. In an annexe built specially to receive it is the skeleton of a great whale, eighty-seven feet long, washed ashore on the west coast a few years ago. One pathetic and modern treasure is a memento of Captain Scott's expedition—a small silken New Zealand flag, a combination of the Union Jack and the Southern Cross—worked for Dr. Wilson by a Christchurch lady. The flag was stitched to his shirt and went with him to the South Pole and was brought back by the relief party.

Christchurch has an Art Gallery with a small permanent collection of paintings, and in it exhibitions are held of Arts and Crafts—pictures, wood-carving, bookbinding or embroidery—to encourage local talent; also a theatre, music halls and picture-palaces, and halls for dances and lectures. In one big hall was held, while I was staying in Christchurch, a series of the "Dominion Literary and Musical Competitions." They lasted for several weeks; and men, women and children from all parts of the Dominion, "from Auckland to the Bluff," came to compete in singing, instrumental music, recitations and impromptu speeches; the judges were well-known men from Melbourne, and the general public was admitted. Many of the songs and recitations were excellent, and all were rendered without shyness or hesitation.

There are delightful homes in and around Christchurch—houses large and small, always with some garden-space; and on the outskirts, many of the houses have large gardens, excellently planned and cared for. Sometimes the larger houses are of brick; but as a rule, private houses are of wood and have roofs of corrugated iron; though some newer roofs are of curved Marseilles tiles, or of flat red tiles made in New Zealand. Every house has its outside verandah, used all the year round as a sitting room, and often in summer as a bedroom too.

In the hot weather it is easy to leave Christchurch, either for the mountains or the coast. Many residents have little wooden cottages or huts at the foot of the Port Hills, where there is a wonderful beach of smooth grey sand running northwards in a forty mile curve. Others seek recreation in fishing up one of the rivers of the Canterbury Plain.

Always the holiday may be taken in the open air to an extent which in England is seldom possible.

CHAPTER VIII

FROM CHRISTCHURCH TO THE WEST COAST

At 8.30 one autumn morning, I left Christchurch, the City of the Plains, to travel across New Zealand from the Pacific Ocean to the Tasman Sea. The railway line runs westward through the great Canterbury Plain, a fertile country containing some of the best land in New Zealand for all kinds of farming. Long ago this plain must have been covered with bush, for early settlers tell how in ploughing they used to find the decayed stumps of forest trees; now, on either side of the railway line, are fields of grass or ploughed land—"paddocks," as they are uniformly termed—paddocks of many acres, divided from one another by green hedges of hawthorn or gorse. Scattered among them are homesteads and farm buildings, all usually of wood with iron roofs, and round about the homesteads are gardens, with fruit trees, poplars, drooping willows, oaks or sycamores, the tall dark-foliaged "pinus insignis" from North America, and the bright green sturdy "macrocarpa" pine from California. Often, too, you pass a grove of Australian gums, the clean grey trunks of the full-grown trees erect amid an undergrowth of young blue-grey leaves.

There are flourishing little townships along the line, often bearing familiar English names, such as Malvern or Sheffield. Forty miles from Christchurch, the plain begins gradually to give way to low hills, outliers of the distant Southern Alps; and after winding up among them for another twenty miles the train reaches Cass, the terminus. At Cass passengers are transferred to coaches drawn by horses, which take them over the mountain pass dividing Canterbury from Westland.

It is a wonderful mountain drive of twenty-six miles, and will in a few years' time be superseded by the new railway line which is to connect Cass with the West Coast by way of the Otira tunnel. This tunnel is a difficult piece of engineering work, boring five miles through the mountain and under a river bed. So far, only two and a half miles of it is finished. Coach road and railway line follow the course of a wide river bed, an expanse of rough grey shingle and big stones, at its widest a mile across. The river was just now a deep narrow stream in the middle of the stones, but in flood it becomes a mighty and swift-flowing torrent. We forded the stream without difficulty, the water only reaching to the horses' knees. Then on up another valley beside another wide shingly river, which became a narrow mountain stream as we followed its course. High bush-covered hills were on either side, so high that at three in the afternoon we drove in shadow, and watched the sunlight shining on the opposite ranges. All along this valley are scattered the huts of the men employed on the line, some of them tiny "wharés" of calico stretched over a wooden framework, with chimneys of corrugated iron or wood; better dwellings made of wood roofed with iron, and usually only one small window; and there was one smart house with a verandah—in this the chief engineer had been living. Bonny children were playing about, and in the centre of the railwaymen's township was the school with the school-mistress's cottage—both of wood painted red.

We could see the entrance to the Otira tunnel on the hillside above us, and soon we began the ascent of the pass, up a steep winding road, and on reaching the summit, two thousand feet above sea-level, left Canterbury behind us, and descended by an even steeper road down into Westland. The Otira Gorge is far-famed, and tourists come many miles to see it. Mountains covered with forest tower up on either side, sombre and magnificent; in front are still higher mountains, their snowy summits glittering in the sunshine, and far away at the bottom of the ravine flows the Otira river, a brawling mountain torrent. Ever the road winds steadily down, cut from the hillside, in places supported on stays of wood or iron driven into the rock, and at some places dangerously insecure, where the face of the cliff consists only of loose rubble, and the road has no solid foundation, and is liable to disappear after storm and flood. There had been a slip only a few weeks before, but the new track was safe enough as we drove over it; the five horses were driven quickly, too, at a sharp trot all the way. The forest on the eastern slope of the pass is almost entirely of beech trees—tall and graceful, with small, glossy, green leaves, evergreen for the most part, and which remain on the trees through the winter, though in autumn some of them turn yellow or red. On the western side are beeches too, but among them grow many pines and other trees: the ferns and mosses are more luxuriant than on the eastern slopes, while here and there you catch sight of a waterfall rushing down a steep crag among the trees.

From Otira township a two hours' journey by train takes the traveller on to Greymouth, which is reached just twelve hours after leaving Christchurch.

Greymouth is a small township situated on the coast, built upon level land at the mouth of the Grey River, which is wide enough to serve as a harbour for ships of fair size, principally cargo boats. The bar outside is sometimes so rough that ships can neither enter nor leave, and Greymouth people would be glad of half a million pounds with which to construct a better harbour. Most of the houses are of wood and iron, the shops have outside verandahs, and the roofs are usually painted red. There is a church of grey stone with a spire, and other churches of less imposing appearance; a large red brick post-office with a tall clock tower, as well as several banks and hotels. Forty years ago, when gold was found in abundance all along the west coast, Greymouth was a gayer and more thriving town than it is to-day. It is now a coal mining centre and a market for dairy produce.

Next day I left Greymouth, and went on by train to Hokitika, twenty-eight miles away, travelling through the bush all the time. There are clearings at intervals, with some sawmills at work, and in other parts cattle and sheep grazing, and round Hokitika is plenty of open country suitable for farmland.

Hokitika is just such another town as Greymouth, but smaller, with a population of between two and three thousand. It, too, has houses with red roofs, banks and hotels. In addition it has a fine clock tower, set in an open space, and is the proud possessor of a Carnegie Library of solid stone; in the reading room of the Library I looked at a London *Graphic* only six weeks old. Hokitika is only a few miles from Kumara, the home of Mr. Dick Seddon, the late Premier, and Hokitika and the West Coast generally owe a great deal to his interest in their welfare.

Twelve miles from Hokitika, away to the east, is a lake called Lake Kanieri, which I had been told was beautiful, so next morning I hired a horse and went for a twelve mile ride along a road through the forest in search of it. I found it well worth seeing—a lake five miles long and two wide, surrounded on all sides by forest, hills behind hills at the head of the lake, the most distant streaked with snow. It was a dull day, with a strong wind blowing from the lake, and the yellow-grey waves came dashing against the shore in a line of white surf, like the breakers of some inland sea. The distant mountains were deep purple, an intense, almost black shade, toning into the dark green of the nearer hills.

From Hokitika the train took me on for another twenty miles to Ross. I arrived there at sunset, a glorious sunset over the sea—all crimson and gold—which turned Ross into an enchanted city of grey mist, surrounded by low hills and trees bathed in a pink glow.

Ross is a little town of seven hundred inhabitants, but it is brilliantly lighted by electricity, and boasts four churches—Anglican, Roman Catholic, Presbyterian and Wesleyan—and it has seven public houses.

My further journey of seventy miles south was in the mail coach, drawn by a team of four horses. We set forth at seven-thirty in a grey dawn, which soon changed to a day of brilliant sunshine.

Just outside Ross is a gold mine, worked by electricity, on the latest and most improved American methods. The power is brought twenty-five miles from a waterfall near Kanieri Lake. Great things are hoped from this mine, but at present there is so much water in the workings that most of the time is taken up with pumping out some millions of gallons a day. Beyond the mine we saw a gold sluicing claim, with long wooden troughs running down from the hill side. A great force of water is brought through an iron hose-pipe and directed against the rocks, which it tears down; the fragments of earth fall into the wooden troughs, the sand and gravel are washed away, while the gold stays at the bottom.

Very soon we had our last sight of the sea, and for the rest of the way drove through the forest. The West Coast forest extends for three hundred miles between the sea and the Southern Alps, and to the north of the Alps as well—a narrow strip of country varying in width from fifteen to thirty miles, and I think that the further south you go the more beautiful it becomes. It is a semi-tropical forest in appearance, with its countless groves of tall and slender tree-ferns, with their rough brown stems and thick heads of drooping feathery fronds, a yard and more in length, and with its amazingly luxuriant undergrowth of trailing creepers and lianes, while daintiest ferns, mosses and lichens grow everywhere round and upon the forest trees. The Westland forest trees are mighty giants, and chief among them is the red pine or "rimu," as the Maoris call it. This tree towers straight up to a height of a hundred feet or so, then it branches out into a head of thick stems, becoming quite slender at their tips, and drooping gracefully towards the ground, clothed with long, coppery-green tassels, hardly leaves at all, but green scales packed closely together, and giving the tree the effect of being dressed in a "gay green gown" of shaggy moss. Then there is the white pine, growing best in swampy places, its enormous trunk buttressed like the clustered pillars of a mighty church, at first bare, and then showing dense tufts of green bristly spines high up against the sky; the black pine too, with grey trunk and very dark green spines. Less tall than the pines is the red birch or beech — the names are interchangeable in Westland — its leaves the size of elm-tree leaves, but thicker and more glossy, and all the branches now bearing bunches of dead, brown flowers. Of the same size as the beech is the "miro," a tree with smaller but equally glossy leaves, and berries beloved of the New Zealand wood pigeon. The "totara" is a tree that reminds one of the English yew, but its narrow leaves are longer and of a yellower green. Enormous "rata" trees grow in this bush, their branches thickly covered with myrtle-shaped leaves; the crimson flower was quite over on the big trees, but on the rata-vine which drapes many of the forest trees were still patches of red blossom among the green. Close to the road were giant fuchsia trees, with either yellow leaves or bare branches, for the fuchsia is one of the few trees that sheds its leaves in winter.

One of the strangest trees is the lancewood, which, when young, bears long narrow leaves like lances, pointing stiffly to the ground; after some years' growth, the leaves become broader and shorter and no longer point downwards, they grow straight out or point towards the sky. Other New Zealand trees have this curious habit of bearing different kinds of leaves at different stages of their growth, and botanists see in it a reminiscence of the changes that the plants' ancestors have lived through — varying leaves suited to variations in the climate.

The New Zealand bush is for the most part a sombre forest of many shades of green; though now the fuchsia is yellow, and the pepper-tree's leaves are green and pink; while in spring the clematis festoons the bush with masses of starry white blossoms; in summer the rata blazes crimson, tree-veronicas and olearias show purple and white, and the ribbon-wood bears the loveliest clusters of fragile white flowers. When the sun shines, you forget that you ever thought the bush sombre, so enchanting is the effect of light and shade on stem and leaf. Shafts of sunlight glint through the forest as through the aisles of some vast cathedral, bringing into strong relief the waving light-green fronds of stately tree-ferns, making a glorious harmony of green and gold, "all glossy glooms and shifting sheen."

There is very little bare space in the Westland bush: all the plants grow close together, struggling for their share of sunlight and air; creepers climb to the tops of trees, and hang down in long festoons; plants with long, lily-like leaves perch among the branches, and sometimes hide the whole trunk with their drooping greenery. Ferns of many species cover the ground and live high up on the trees, and such lovely ferns they are: some have bright, glossy fronds from six to eight feet long; there is bracken, tall, with thick wiry leaves; or short and fragile, its fronds like the most delicate green lace. The ferns that live on the tree-trunks have usually short fronds, but sometimes they are over a foot in length; the polypods are thick and shining, the "filmy" ferns of such delicate texture that you can almost see through them. The kidney fern, "trichomanes reniforme," is one of these transparent ferns and grows in great abundance on the trees; it is shaped in exact accordance with its name, and has its spores arranged round the edge of the frond like a neat brown frill. There are beautiful club mosses trailing over the ferns and draping the banks by the roadside with garlands of bronze and green; and painted in for the ground colour are green mosses and grey lichens, all shades of grey and green with touches of copper; and on smooth banks coral red berries lying among the mosses.

THE WESTLAND FOREST.

Every few miles we came to homesteads and clearings, where the bush has been cut down and burnt, and grass sown for grazing; the ground is too cold and damp for corn, but grass grows well and sheep and cattle thrive. It seems sad to destroy such beautiful forest, but settlers cannot make a living out of the bush, and as Government is wisely keeping two or three chains of forest all along the road on either side as well as other big areas of forest country, there is no fear that the bush will entirely disappear before the settler's axe.

During our seventy mile drive, we crossed several rivers and creeks; only three of the rivers are bridged, the others must be forded; it was easy work, as the rivers were low, but in flood time they become roaring torrents, rushing over wide river-beds filled with big boulders and rough shingle, and many lives have been lost in the attempt to cross. From all the open spaces we had lovely views of distant mountains, deep blue behind the green tints of nearer trees, and often tall rimus standing out from the forest, bronze tassels against a background of blue. It is not a level road all the way—at one point I got down and walked on up a hill between three and four miles, and looking back had a wonderful view over the valley. I stood among the trees at the top, looking down upon the forest stretching away for miles in billowy curves to right and left, a blue haze over its greenness; and beyond, in the far background, a mountain crowned with snow.

We passed three charming lakes, each one many acres in extent, and all with trees right down to the water's edge, the ground rising away from the water in gentle slopes. From the hill above one of these lakes, we saw the snowy peaks of Tasman and Cook, fifty miles away. On swampy land grows the New Zealand flax (phormium tenax), which is now being exported in some quantity to Japan for use in the manufacture of silk, and to Ireland to be used in making linen.

At 1 p.m. on the second day after leaving Ross, we came to the end of our journey—a solitary hotel, nestling under the mountains; and the driver pointed out to me with pride the Franz Josef Glacier, coming grandly down between the mountains to meet the forest, only three miles from the hotel.

CHAPTER IX
THREE WEEKS IN WESTLAND

South Westland is a land apart from the rest of New Zealand—cut off by the mountains—an enchanted land, which if you once learn to know and love you never wish to leave, and when you do go away, you must always be wanting to return. It is a land of mountain and forest, of glacier and waterfall and rushing river, of blue sky and wide ocean. I first saw it in late autumn, when day after day the sun shone with steady radiance, warming you through and through as if it were still summer; bell-birds and tuis called to one another in the trees, and merry fantails darted hither and thither in the sun, catching sandflies, and spreading out their tails of brown or black-and-white stripes, like miniature fans. The district has a yearly rainfall of over a hundred inches, and to this owes the extreme luxuriance of its forests and the beauty of its many streams. It is a different world from the Alpine region on the east, where the mountains are grand with a grandeur of snowy summit and bare brown rock, and trees are few and stunted. In Westland you see the same peaks of snow, but they rise behind ranges clad in stately forests, shrouded often in mysterious violet tints; the glaciers which fall steeply down the mountain sides are bordered by tall trees; in summer the crimson rata blooms against the snow, and in May little white orchids were in flower only a few feet from the ice.

I went to Waiho Gorge intending to spend a week there, but stayed for three, and the following year I returned and remained for two months. The hotel stands in a cleared space in the forest, on a gentle slope overlooking the Waiho river valley—a wide flat with grass and trees. The Franz Josef Glacier is three miles away, and the road to it is no rough and stony track, but a moss-grown path through bush of more than usual loveliness. Here the sunlight, filtering through interlacing branches, shines on great cushions of green moss, on the rich green fronds of many crape ferns with curling feathery tips, and everywhere soil and tree-stems alike are clothed with ferns, lichens, liverworts and mosses in bewildering profusion and most satisfying beauty.

The Franz Josef Glacier is three-quarters of a mile wide and eight miles long, and flows to within six hundred feet of sea level, it is fed by another smaller glacier, and by vast snowfields lying among the mountains at its head. Its bed is far steeper than the Tasman, and the rate of flow much quicker, so the surface changes continually, and is broken up into the most extraordinary ridges and pinnacles of every conceivable shape and size; the pinnacles stand up like great teeth of ice, crevasses vary in depth from ten feet to a hundred, and the narrow ridges between are often cut short by other crevasses at right angles, making climbing among them tedious and difficult. A few years ago a hanging gallery of wooden steps on iron staples was erected in the hillside near the terminal face, forty feet above the level of the glacier; within six months the glacier rose up in a gigantic ice-wave and tore down the gallery like a child's toy; it then began to subside, and, when I saw it, was almost at its former level; but the gallery has not been replaced, and a few tattered planks still hang from the cliff.

The Franz Josef is almost free from moraine, though there are a few grey rocks and stones and coarse silt scattered about on the ice above the terminal face, which in the centre of the glacier is a sheer ice-wall, two hundred feet high. The Waiho River rises here, in an amphitheatre of blue and white ice, sometimes at one point, sometimes at another; great blocks of ice are constantly breaking away at the snout, and the river escapes wherever it can force its way. The ice of the Franz Josef has the most beautiful colouring; there are caves of clearest crystal, or of white ice faintly tinged with blue, and many moulins and ice-bridges of an intense, bright blue. From Waiho, the Franz Josef forms the nearest highway across the Alps into Canterbury—a long climb up the glacier and over the snowy saddle at its head, then down the steep slope of another glacier to the Tasman.

On my first visit, under the careful guidance of a Westland guide whose home is at Waiho, and who knows and loves the glacier and mountains as his intimate friends, I explored the lower slopes of the Franz Josef. We went together as far up the glacier as a hut which had just been built, three hours' climb from the terminal face.

At this point a rocky mountain spur juts out into the glacier—Cape Defiance it is aptly named—and on this spur, some few hundred feet above the glacier, a little platform has been levelled, and a hut of wood and iron put up. It is like the hut by the Hooker Glacier on the other side of the Alps, and is divided by a wooden partition into two rooms, with six bunks in each room, but instead of an oil stove, the Cape Defiance Hut has an open fireplace made of flat grey stones from the mountain side. The hut is perfectly fitted together; and every strip of corrugated iron and wood used in it has been carried on men's backs up the glacier in loads of fifty to sixty pounds—there is no other way, and the two men who did it all needed to be mountaineers as well as carpenters.

This hut was put up at Government expense, it is provisioned and kept going by private enterprise, and the guiding in Westland is in private hands.

Round the hut grow ferns and a bushy tangle of ribbon-wood, broom and coprosma trees, and from its windows you look up towards the head of the glacier or across to the mountains on the opposite side, and on the far side of a small tributary glacier behind Cape Defiance, you hear a waterfall thundering down from a height of a thousand feet. The first winter snow had fallen and the whole glacier was covered with fresh snow, making walking easier over the slippery ice, but as we climbed higher the snow was deeper—almost up to my knees—and when after sunset we reached the hut, we found it half-buried in snow, with snow-drifts two or three feet deep all round it.

The snow was speedily shovelled away, and a cheerful log fire soon blazed on the open hearth.

At eight o'clock that night the moon rose, full and brilliant, and from the door of the hut we saw glacier and mountains distinct in the moonlight: at our feet the full width of the glacier, its uneven edges stretching upwards to a great ice-fall of white and towering pinnacles, its lower slopes vanishing into the night: meeting the snow of the glacier was the fresh white snow of the mountains rising from it—an unbroken expanse of snow low down, but above a mingling of brown rock and whiteness against the blue sky, and the blue was a deep violet shade, changing to sapphire where the clear moon shone serenely. Very few stars were visible, but one planet gleamed like a lamp over the crest of the mountain opposite, and above our heads shone the Southern Cross—the five stars of the cross guarded by two bright pointers, shining even more brilliantly than the Cross itself—while over the glacier, behind the topmost pinnacles, floated a few soft, white, fleecy clouds.

I was the first lady to sleep in the Cape Defiance Hut, and found my bunk most comfortable with mattress and blankets, and for pillow, a spare blanket slipped inside a pillow-slip. I was offered a hot water bottle, but declined that, and though water in my room froze during the night, I was perfectly warm.

Next morning before I got up my guide brought me a cup of tea and a biscuit, then hot water in a billy for me to wash in. For breakfast I had a poached egg served on hot buttered toast, and cups of delicious coffee—and all these luxuries on the edge of a glacier!

The snow was too deep for us to go higher on the glacier, so we climbed a short way up the mountain behind the hut, where we found a convenient bare patch, sheltered by an overhanging rock, and could sit down on the rucksack and study the view.

We were only two thousand feet above sea level, and there in front of us was the Tasman Sea, its irregular coastline sixteen miles distant; the sea was a smooth grey, backed by level grey and yellow clouds—a quiet, lonely sea, and on its surface no faintest trace of fishing boat or steamer.

Just within the coastline glimmered the waters of a peaceful lagoon, and to the right, among the trees, shone a large lake, the surface ruffled by wind, which gave the effect of a fringe of snow on the far side. Between the foot of the glacier and the sea flowed the Waiho River, blue amid the pearly shingle of its wide bed. There is flat land sparsely covered with rough grass and shrub on both sides of the Waiho, then between river and sea stretch ridge behind ridge of low bush-covered hills, the furthest jutting out steeply into the ocean.

Beyond the glacier, on the opposite side to where we sat, lies a long level ridge, densely clothed with forest trees, and over them lay the snow gradually melting in the hot sun. Behind the wooded range are higher mountains, and at right angles to them, covering the lower levels, are miles of forest, deep green at first, paling through greens and greys to dimmest grey, where the line of forest meets the dim, grey sea.

FRANZ JOSEF AND ALMER GLACIERS FROM CAPE DEFIANCE.

Looking up the glacier, we could see two rocky peaks which stand some miles above the head, but not the actual head of the glacier, or the snowfield which feeds it. As we saw it that morning the Franz Josef was one magnificent ice-fall—the topmost ridge of huge ice-crags sharply outlined against the blue, and then a steep descent of rough broken ice, and over all a spotless mantle of snow, white and glistening in the sunshine: mountain and glacier and snow-sprinkled forests combined to make one glorious scene of wintry splendour.

Back to the hut for an early lunch, after which we washed plates and cups, swept the floor, folded up the blankets, sorted out the provisions, put out the fire with a sprinkling of snow, and with key in the lock outside, we left the hut to its winter solitude.

Twenty miles from the Franz Josef Glacier is another, the Fox, which is eleven miles long, and this too, like the Franz Josef, comes down among the forest and ends in a winding river.

To reach the Fox glacier, I rode on horseback through the bush, down the "Main South Road"—such a pretty road—worn bare in places by waggons and horses' feet, but for the most part soft with grass and moss, with grassy margins bordering the forest. After about eight miles, the road becomes a mere track, steep and often stony, and across it are cut shallow water-courses, lined with stones and the stems of tree-ferns; the whole road is continually being improved and widened, and in a few years settlers will be able to drive a carriage where they must now either ride or walk. At intervals by the side of the track are huts, usually of corrugated iron: one was of logs roofed with shingles, and one of fern stems, and along a section on which several men were working, we saw tents of canvas or white calico. The permanent iron huts are put up at Government expense, for the use primarily of surveyors, gold prospectors or roadmen, but any traveller is at liberty to light a fire and spend the night in one of them. At one such hut, standing in a grass paddock, fenced in with barbed wire, we dismounted, turned the horses loose to feed and walked in: it was a small, one-roomed hut, and had four wooden bunks stocked with straw and bracken for bedding, a wide open fireplace, and two wooden benches. We soon had a good fire of dry logs, and when the billy boiled we made tea, and ate our lunch in the sunny paddock, surrounded by bush-covered hills and the remoteness of the forest world.

The aloofness of the "back blocks" is amazing, so vast and yet so friendly; in the forest itself you have only the birds for company, and they are all fearless and trustful, and unsuspecting of any danger from stick or gun: sometimes near a homestead you see cows or sheep grazing by tracks or river-beds, but the only native four-footed animals in all New Zealand are two varieties of bats, and its forests have no snakes or hurtful creatures of any kind. The people, too, who live among the Westland forests, share in the friendliness of the forest birds; even alone on a bush track at night, I always felt quite sure that if I did meet anyone—roadman or surveyor—he would simply be very glad to see me and would do anything in his power to help me.

The Main South Road goes up three steep hills and down into the valleys between, over rivers and creeks, and always it is a forest road, and we looked through brown trunks and twining lianes and waving fern-fronds upon trees of every shade of green, down in the valleys and up the hillsides, and often some glorious snowy peak crowning the forest. Wherever the hill has been cut away in making the track the once bare soil is covered with ferns and mosses. We rode by walls of green flecked with red, where long glossy ferns and trailing festons of lycopodiums, all copper and green, stretched out to touch us as we passed; and down the cliffs tumbled sparkling waterfalls to join the brawling streams below. At sunset, we came to the brow of a long steep hill, overlooking a wide fertile plain — two silvery rivers winding through it; in the distance low bush-hills, and over them as the sun went down, a pink haze, through which the dark trees showed as through a filmy transparency, in front of a clear sky, blue tinged with green.

At Weheka, the homestead where we stayed, I learnt a little about life in remote places: here we were eighty-seven miles from train or doctor, but always, through the telephone, in touch with the world outside. When anyone is ill, the doctor is rung up at Ross or Hokitika, and symptoms are described, and remedies are sent by the next mail — a doctor's visit costs forty or fifty pounds, and in case of emergency each settler must be his own doctor. For children in these country districts Government provides "household schools," allowing £6 a head per annum for three or more children of school age, and a teacher is sent from the nearest school, or sometimes the mother of the children is the teacher; when there are as many as seven children to be taught, a schoolroom is built for them near the homestead, and desks and maps are provided.

Round Weheka a good deal of land has been cleared and sown with grass, and our host was shortly sending two hundred bullocks to the market at Hokitika, over a hundred miles away.

This farmhouse grows every year more modern and up-to-date. The original homestead was a small one-roomed hut planted in the forest.

The present house is roomy and comfortable, with large sitting-room and many bedrooms, the kitchen is a big room apart from the rest, and yet another building is the bathroom, in which is a large bath and a cold water tap, and near all the rest is the Government school. When I first stayed at Weheka, music was provided by an excellent gramophone, but the following year I found a new piano, and one daughter was learning to play the piano, and another the violin.

At first the house was lighted by oil lamps and candles, now electric light has been installed, and an electric globe greets you at the garden-gate. There is only one other house near the homestead, but the Main South Road goes on bravely for thirteen miles to the next house, and beyond that to another settlement fifty miles further south.

The day following my arrival at Weheka, I was taken on the Fox Glacier.

Compared with the Franz Josef the Fox Glacier carries a quantity of moraine, the terminal face slopes gently down to the valley, and above it are boulders and stones, of every size; many of them are covered with bright red lichen, which makes them look as though they had been sprinkled with brick-dust. The lower ice is in smooth layers, and when you have safely crossed the tempestuous Fox River and scrambled over the loose rubble of the moraine, walking on the glacier itself presents no difficulty.

At one time this glacier stood at a far higher level, and one high rock-face has deep grooves worn in it by the stones carried down in distant ages. Under the rock with its deep grooves, the ice has been forced into huge curves through the variation in its rate of flow: the centre of the glacier moves most quickly, and the ice at the edge has been left behind and wedged against the mountain side: in its efforts to move on, the ice river has become twisted into the strangest contortions, and you can trace cause and effect with unmistakeable clearness.

From a point only a mile up we had a splendid view towards the head of the glacier. Ridges of rock and snow stand above it, and on their right is one tall white peak, beyond which the glacier rises and curves round in a sweeping ice-fall of pinnacles, all jagged white ice shot with green. Looking back down the valley, we saw the sea lying in grey streaks on the distant horizon.

Forest and ice meet at the glacier's edge; we boiled ice-water in the billy, and sat on a grey pebbly beach, under the shelter of a big tree-veronica.

The day had been grey and gloomy, but at sunset, as we left the glacier, the sun shone out, first lighting up the yellow autumn leaves of the fuchsia trees as from the glow of a fiery furnace, then flooding all the forest with golden light, so that for a few minutes all the bush was turned to gold, with the glacier behind part white and part grey shadow, until the sun sank below the horizon, and all was grey.

CHAPTER X

THROUGH THE BULLER VALLEY

I first went into Westland from Christchurch by way of the Otira Gorge: I left it for Wellington by way of the Buller Gorge and the town of Nelson. For three days the return journey is the same—the drive by coach to Ross and the railway to Greymouth: here, instead of turning east to cross the mountains, you go on still by railway, over the Grey River and into the province of Nelson as far as Reefton, where at present the line ends, though it is gradually being continued further north. Motor cars meet the train and take passengers on for the remaining fifty miles between Reefton and Westport, running for a great part of the journey through the Buller Gorge, close to the Buller River.

It is a very fine river, from two to three chains wide, and a great volume of brown water flows swiftly between high tree-covered cliffs. There is very little room for the road, which in places has been cut on the face of the cliff overhanging the river, and now on the opposite side trees are being felled and the beauty of the river injured to make a way for the new railroad. There is a certain sameness in the scenery, beautiful though it undoubtedly is—mile after mile of rounded hills of varying height, all uniformly covered with luxuriant growth of pines, beeches, fuchsias, veronicas and tree-ferns, and ever the brown river flowing below.

Westport is the centre of the coal-mining industry—a small and dreary town of wooden houses and straight streets, at the head of a desolate plain backed by low forest-hills. It has a harbour at the mouth of the Buller, and here I watched trucks being unloaded into the hold of a small steamer. It was a most scientific unlading—the crane hoisted up the loaded truck and kept it suspended over the hold, then the bottom of the truck opened, and all the coal came tumbling out exactly as it was wanted.

After one night at Westport, a motor coach took me back through the Buller Gorge and on up the Buller Valley, until twenty-seven miles from Westport it left me at a small hotel; here I had lunch, and afterwards went on again in a coach drawn by four sleek and well-groomed horses. All that afternoon we drove by the side of the Buller River, and all the time the scenery was fine—high cliffs and dense forests, and sometimes through a break in the cliffs we saw a high distant mountain peak, white with freshly fallen snow. The river-bed has been very rich in gold, and some is still found, though the claims are now not worked very energetically; one sluicing hose, that should have been at work tearing down the rock, was aimlessly pouring water with great force back into the river.

It was the end of May and cold—as the driver sympathetically remarked "too late in the season for the Buller." I was very glad to see the first twenty miles, but after that, I wearied of forest and cliff; there was too much scenery endlessly repeated, and I was too cold to enjoy it.

The last few miles we drove in the dark, and finally came to a little township in an open valley, and here stayed for the night.

This valley and the hills surrounding it are all being cleared for grazing land, and up to the very tops of the hills are blackened tree-trunks, while grass is springing up everywhere round the half-burnt stumps.

For another ten miles beyond the little settlement the road still follows the course of the Buller, which is now a narrow mountain stream of dark green water, hurrying along between high wooded banks, until at last—and I rejoiced in the change—it branches off, and up another valley and over a low saddle to Glenhope, another small settlement, where we again reach a railway and are able to proceed by train to Nelson.

After travelling for two days through a wild and for the most part uninhabited country, the town of Nelson and the smiling fertility of the hollow in which it lies come as a complete and happy surprise. All round Nelson the land is highly cultivated, with hop-gardens and fruit orchards, and though the nearer hills have lost their forest growth and are bare of all but grass, the town itself is lavishly planted with many trees, the berberis hedges were a mass of crimson leaf, and yellow cassias and wattles were flowering, even in mid-winter.

Nelson is known in this land of sunshine as "Sunny Nelson," and now that a private donor has generously given a site, there is presently to be built here a Solar Observatory, from which scientists may study the sun.

The town has eight thousand inhabitants, good hotels and shops, and fine wide streets; a museum too, and public flower gardens. On rising ground among the trees at the head of the main street—Trafalgar Street—stands the Anglican Cathedral, of wood, painted red; it has a shingle roof and tapering spire, and a broad flight of white stone steps leads up to it: they are very handsome steps, but look a little incongruous so close to the wooden walls.

There is a big jam factory at which fruit is tinned and a great deal of excellent jam made: there is no temptation to adulterate the jams, as fruit comes to the factory in greater quantity than the makers can use—peaches, nectarines, apricots, plums, strawberries or quinces—one of the men told me that quince jam is the only kind they are ever asked to send to England: in New Zealand, where quinces grow in such abundance that they are often left to rot on the ground, it is a jam of little account.

In the main, Nelson is a delightful residential town, with good schools and plenty of pleasant houses standing in pretty gardens.

Only a mile from the town is the port and the open sea, and by the sand dunes of a wide bay cottages are being built by the people of Nelson, and here they come and picnic, and enjoy sea bathing and golf and wonderful views across the bay, of snowy mountains and blue hills. The hills have as foreground a wide stretch of open country, neither hilly nor flat, but crumpled into little ridges running in all directions. This crumpled land is the district of Moutere, and here it has recently been discovered that apples grow better than they do anywhere else in the neighbourhood, so all who have land there are turning it to account for apple orchards.

The great excitement of the place just then was the visit to the port of H.M.S. "New Zealand."

Hundreds of people went aboard and were shown the ship and many of her treasures—such as signed portraits of the King and Queen, hanging on either side of a glass case containing presents given to the ship—silver gilt cups, massive branched candlesticks and Maori curios; portraits too of Dick Seddon and Sir Joseph Ward.

Officers and men were entertained in the town, and the sailors gave exhibitions of naval drill and sports in a large paddock near the port.

June 3rd, the King's birthday, is observed through the Dominion as a general holiday.

It was winter certainly, but the sun shone and the air was mild, and friends took me out picnicing. First we drove three miles in an open carriage to a reservoir on the outskirts of the town, from there a steep track took us into the bush, and by a trickling stream we piled up sticks and boiled the billy, and then sat down for tea on a mossy bank overlooking a wooded ravine. It was all very pleasant and a little unexpected at that time of year, but other picnic parties were doing the same.

From Nelson steamers run to Wellington.

Nelson is situated at the north of South Island, and Wellington at the extreme southern point of North Island, but between the two places lie many miles of coastline, and the voyage takes several hours—from early morning until late at night, if as on the day when I crossed Cook Strait, the steamer calls in at Picton. Between Nelson and Picton the land shows a very curious geological formation—a flat tableland cut through by deep gorges up which the sea flows in long curving arms, and all the arms or "sounds" are indented with numberless bays, large and small, and off the coast and within the sounds are many rocky, tree-clad islands.

At the entrance to Pelorus Sound the boats have for many years been met by a white dolphin—Pelorus Jack—who always escorted them up to Picton. Jack was specially protected by Act of Parliament, but for over a year nothing has been seen of him, and his old friends fear that he is dead.

The steamer hugs the coast and you admire the high cliffs and forests and the waterways that separate them. We turned up Queen Charlotte Sound—a narrow entrance and then a long landlocked harbour, up which it took two hours to steam. On either side were high bush hills, cleared in places for grass; round us played a large shoal of porpoises, the great creatures often jumping right out of the water close to the ship, while all the time grey gulls circled gracefully round and round.

At Picton we found H.M.S. "New Zealand" again on view, anchored behind a small island at the head of the sound; the town was crowded with people who had come to see her and join in the festivities, and outside the Town Hall were decorations of tree-ferns and feathery rimu branches.

That evening we had a calm and uneventful journey down the sound, then suddenly as the ship entered Cook Strait, she lurched over, and continued to roll and pitch for the next two hours.

I think most of the passengers were glad to be at peace and safely berthed in Wellington Harbour.

CHAPTER XI
THE COPLAND PASS

As seen from the Hermitage, the Southern Alps form an apparently impassable barrier between Canterbury on the east and the Province of Westland lying between the mountains and the western sea. There are certainly no coach roads or bridle tracks across the snow, but with the help of a guide, a good walker, however inexperienced in mountaineering, can without much difficulty cross the mountains by one of the passes or saddles which divide some of the high peaks. Accordingly, early in April, I was ready to cross the Copland Pass with a guide who was returning to Westland—the same guide who last year took me on the Franz Josef glacier.

Among the mountains the weather is always an uncertain quantity, and the day fixed for leaving the Hermitage was hopelessly wet, so we had to wait. The next day was fine, so in the afternoon we started and walked along the track for seven miles up the valley to the Hooker Hut, hoping to spend one night there and go on next day. All that night rain poured in torrents and the wind howled round the hut in furious gusts. Now this hut with its framework of wood looks very fragile, and as it rocked and shook me in my bunk all night I wondered would it stand the strain. I was assured in the morning that it was built on very solid foundations and anchored firmly to the rock, and not at all likely to be blown over. That day and the following night the wind and rain continued, so we left the hut and tramped back to the Hermitage and there stayed for another two days.

On a beautiful sunshiny afternoon we tried again, and as we walked up to the hut, Mount Cook shone pink in the evening glow, the sky behind the mountains and away southwards down the Tasman Valley was blue and clear, with a few dainty clouds, and there seemed every prospect of fine weather. During the night up sprang the wind, and it was blowing hard as we left the hut to have a look at the pass. From the Hooker Hut a rough track leads up and over the tops of rocky ridges, where sometimes there is no track at all, but you must climb with hands as well as feet, and on this particular day the wind was so strong that I could only just manage to stand or breathe, and was glad to be securely roped to my guide and know that if I did fall it would not be far. After two hours' climbing, we had sleet driving against our faces to contend with as well as wind, and higher up a snowstorm was raging, so back we turned, and were glad to reach the shelter of the hut once more.

Snow fell round the hut during the night, but cleared off the next morning, and soon after nine o'clock we made another start. The day was quite still, hardly a blade of grass moved, masses of white fleecy clouds floated round and above the mountains, and as the sun grew stronger, light mists rose from the valley below us, and scattered like thin gauze among the clouds. The Hermitage showed clearly in the valley, its white wall and red roof in sharp relief against a background of dark green and brown hillside; in front of the Hermitage the wide-stretching grey shingle of the Tasman river-bed, with the river apparently running uphill towards Lake Pukaki, very blue and distinct forty miles away, and having the curious effect of a lake up in the sky; behind the lake, brown mountains sprinkled with snow showing plainly against flat, indigo-coloured clouds, and over all a clear dome of pale blue. Climbing up the track was easy work on such a quiet morning, and we had at first no use for the rope.

After the rock-ridge come snow-slopes, where there is always the possibility of slipping, so the guide put me on the rope and went ahead, kicking steps in the soft snow, or cutting them with his ice-axe where the snow was frozen. We went along the edges of deep crevasses and past lovely ice-caverns, where fringes of glittering icicles guard the entrances to blue recesses in the white ice, and up one short ice wall, where hand holes were cut as well as steps, and I climbed with hands and feet from one step to the next, with the help of my axe stuck firmly in the ledge above.

At twelve o'clock we gained the summit, 7,000 feet above sea level, and found a narrow rock-wall, a succession of sharply toothed rocks, too sharp for snow to lodge on them, standing with their bases in the snow. We stood there, beside the rocky wall, with one hand in Westland and the other in Canterbury. It was now a radiant day of brilliant sunshine and deep blue sky, and we were surrounded by white peaks towering majestically into the blue heaven. Looking back, we had a fine view of Mount Cook and the Mount Cook Range, striking off at right angles to the main Divide. Mount Cook stood at the head, very snowy and beautiful, and the mountains of that range were a series of sharp rocky peaks, with patches of last year's snow on their summits, and a powdery sprinkling of fresh snow reaching far down their sides. Looking along the main Divide to the south, were peaks of rock and snow between us and the whiteness of Mounts Footstool and Sefton. These giants of respectively over nine and ten thousand feet rise up grandly from the valley — their steep, snowy summits glittering in the sunlight, then rough ridges of rock alternating with glacier and snowfield, falling away by degrees to the sheer mountain side of brown rock and sombre green bush. Beyond Sefton and at right angles to the main range were more peaks of rock and snow; facing us were other mountains; far below lay the Copland Valley, a silver stream flowing through it, and behind the brown peaks opposite, half hidden by billowy white clouds, we had a distant glimpse of the blue sea. The whole scene was as fair and wonderful as anyone could wish for.

MOUNTS SEFTON AND FOOTSTOOL FROM COPLAND PASS.

There are higher and grander mountains in other parts of the world, but perhaps none more satisfyingly beautiful than the New Zealand Alps, which always give one a happy feeling that they are exactly right, and could not possibly be altered for the better.

Our next move was the descent into Westland. My guide stood in Canterbury and hauled me over the summit like a sack of potatoes, and then told me to slide down on to a narrow ledge, where I had for my only hand-holds rock thickly glazed with ice; and then to stand upright in snow which, apparently, had no bottom but infinity: not altogether liking the look of it, I rashly said, "I can't," and was answered instantly and very firmly with, "You must." So I had to make the best of it, and with the rope to steady me, found it quite simple after all.

When the guide had scrambled over, he again took the lead, and went forward through the soft snow, kicking steps in a long steep slope, which led us out on a stretch of rough moraine, where fragments of rock of all shapes and sizes, with knife-like edges, lay scattered thickly on the mountain side. You learn to walk cautiously on such rocks, as their sharp edges hurt even through strong boots, and not infrequently one treads on a loose stone, and gets an unexpected tumble and a few bruises. Great boulders succeed the moraine, and here we trod on crisp grass, and found a few late white lilies and mountain daisies still in flower. Concealed by loose stones under a particularly huge boulder were cups and a billy. A fire was soon lighted, and we had an excellent lunch of tea and sardine sandwiches. Over our heads flew a couple of keas in plumage of red and green; beyond a steep precipice close at hand thundered a high and sparkling waterfall, while all round us towered the mountains in solitary grandeur.

One great charm of mountaineering in New Zealand is its loneliness; you feel that for the time the whole world is yours to enjoy—the beauty and the wonder are for you alone.

Right among the Alps there are only two hotels—one on either side—from which it is possible to begin climbing, and if a party sets out to go from one side of the mountains to the other, the fact is known by wire immediately they have started, and news of their arrival is anxiously awaited, and if any delay occurs, an "urgent" telegram is sent round asking for news, so that, wherever you may be, you are always protected by the thoughts of friends from east and west. Not many people have yet discovered the Southern Alps, very few even among the New Zealanders themselves realise how big and marvellous a playground they have in all the Alpine district: in whatever direction you go, you see peaks that no one has yet climbed, and tracts of forest and mountain that are completely unexplored. To climb at all in New Zealand, either on glacier or mountain, you need some share of the spirit of adventure, for you never know at the beginning of the day what you will have done by the end of it; always you must have confidence in your guide, and in your own feet and powers of endurance. There are no planks laid across crevasses or ropes fixed in steep places up the mountains—everything is entirely unspoiled, and the mountains stand as they have done through the centuries before any white man set foot in New Zealand. Until this season there had never been a serious accident to any climber in the Southern Alps, but last

February—on February 22nd, 1914—as an experienced English climber and two of the Hermitage guides were descending Mount Cook, they were overwhelmed by an avalanche, and all three killed, and so sad a disaster has thrown a gloom over all this season's climbing.

From the rock where my guide and I had lunch, a narrow and well-defined track, made only last year, winds gradually down for two or three miles over rough shingle and across many creeks hurrying from the snows. The track leads away down into the valley, winding in and out among the scrub, where snow grass flourishes, waving creamy tassels above thick clumps of long, bright green streamers; and the hillside is dotted with shrubs, gay with brilliant berries in all shades of red and orange. Always from the track are wonderful views of high, bush-covered hills, with snowy peaks ever rising majestically behind the green.

The Alpine plants now give place to the familiar ferns and mosses of the Westland bush, and suddenly the track enters the forest and continues through it for another three miles, sometimes over tree-roots, sometimes leading over rushing torrents where you jump from one boulder to another, but in the main it affords an easy path, until it comes out upon Welcome Flat—a two-mile expanse of open grassy country, with the Copland River running through in many turbulent streams. The streams were too high and swift for me to ford, so my guide took me over on his back, and the water swirled madly round his knees, while I was very safe and quite dry. After the fords we had to leave the river, and strike again into the bush along a disused track, where tree-trunks lay right across the path, bush-lawyers and tree-ferns trailed in our faces, and our feet were entangled in moss-grown roots, and brought up suddenly by deep black hollows, where the wisest course was to sit down and slide from one level to the next. By daylight I am sure this must be an enchanting way through a wealth of forest greenery, but in the dusk and at the end of a long day's tramp it meant a difficult half-hour's scramble, and it was a relief to emerge into the open, and find ourselves at a three-roomed Alpine hut where we stopped for the night.

Close to this hut are pools of hot sulphur water, fed continually by hot springs. The pools lie in an open space amid the bush; trees and ferns and green mosses grow down to the water's edge, and between the separate pools of bubbling green water is a wide deposit of silica in varying shades of pink—emeralds in a setting of garnets—and about the pools, steam constantly rising and floating away over the forest. While the fire was being lighted, soup made and peas boiled for dinner, I had a bath in one of the pools, by the light of a lantern stuck on a convenient post, in delightfully warm water, which kept rising in fresh bubbles all over me as I bathed: a dim moon looked down from a cloudy sky, and all was wrapped in the utter peace and quiet of forest and mountain by night.

The following day was gloomy, wet and disappointing. All round Welcome Flat rise mountains of rock and snow, behind green bush sloping down to the river valleys; I saw no mountains—nothing but trees and valleys below a line of white, impenetrable mist. I was mounted astride on a horse whose back I shared with the packs—bags of sacking filled with rucksack and other bundles, all carefully covered with more sacking to keep them dry. The track leads always through the forest, up and down among the trees, and over many glacier-fed streams—so rough a track that we could only go at a walking pace. When we came to particularly strong and swift-rushing torrents I had to dismount, and, once safe on a big boulder in midstream, I watched admiringly while his master led the horse through the water, and let him scramble up the loose stones of the opposite bank.

At the end of thirteen miles we arrived at a homestead, where it seemed strange to exchange the mountain solitudes for the bustle of farm life, with barking collie dogs, quacking ducks, crowing "roosters," horses, cows and sheep, and people constantly coming and going in and out of a comfortable house, standing in its gay flower-garden, surrounded by green paddocks. We were hungry, and very glad to eat an excellent dinner of roast duck and apple pie, and I was content to rest by a glowing fire and go early to bed.

In the morning, we hired a second horse, and rode the last stage of thirty miles at a good pace, with a long stop at another homestead for lunch. This was a better day than the previous one, part sunny and part gloomy, and I had good views of the mountains. After a few miles, the road—for it is more than a bridle-track just here—leaves the forest and comes out on a wide shingle flat. Among the grey stones a river wanders in many devious branches. Some of the streams were shallow, but one, where the current swirled furiously along, was well over our horses' knees as we forded it. On the further side of the river we stopped, for this is one of the best view-points in all South Westland.

Looking eastward to the mountains, we saw, through floating masses of white cloud, the peaks which I have learnt to know from the other side of the Alps. Haidinger Peak showed square and white against blue sky, and we had fleeting glimpses of Mounts Cook and Tasman—the latter, a sharp snowy peak at the head of the Fox Glacier. Below Mount Tasman the glacier curves down in a broad sweep of white ice, between sombre green forests, towards the river-valleys. From where our horses stood, the wide river-bed—grey shingle with silver streaks of water—made a spacious foreground to the mountains. All about us were low-growing, green shrubs, and tall, feathery, white sprays of "toi-toi" grass. On our left, looking down the river, were low, bush-covered hills, separated by broad gaps, where, only a few miles distant, several rivers flow into the Tasman Sea.

To-day's ride was not lacking in excitement. The previous night there had been a high gale, the telephone wire was down at the fords; and in the forest, trees had been blown across road and wire, one tree so big that it completely blocked the way, and we had to get off our horses. The guide rapidly cut off straggling branches with an axe, which he had brought in case of accidents; we then climbed the trunk, and the horses easily jumped over.

We came safely to our journey's end at Waiho Gorge, by the Franz Josef glacier, at nightfall, greeted cheerily by the light streaming through the open door of the hotel, and by the kindly welcome of my last year's friends.

GLACIER HOTEL, WAIHO GORGE.

CHAPTER XII

THE WESTLAND GLACIERS

I was back at Waiho Gorge and content—seventy miles from the nearest train, and with a mail once a week.

At Waiho, there are a few small huts, three cottages and the hotel. The Glacier Hotel is a two-storied wooden building, with verandah and balcony, and accommodation for between thirty and forty; it has a dining-room, smoking-room and two sitting-rooms, in one of which is an excellent piano; there are two bathrooms with a good supply of hot and cold water, and soon the house will be lighted by electricity—the power to be brought from a convenient waterfall close by. Under the same roof is a store, where you can buy groceries, boot-laces and tobacco, and in the same store you find a post-office with a telephone—that indispensable luxury of the back blocks. It is in the parish of Ross, and four times a year the Anglican clergyman drives seventy miles to hold a service. While I was staying here, the Bishop of Christchurch took a journey of two hundred miles to conduct a Confirmation in the smoking-room: there were nine candidates, some of whom had come more than forty miles. The Presbyterian minister also comes from Ross and holds a service, and sometimes the Roman Catholic priest spends a night at the hotel.

At this hotel, tourists may feel that they are visitors and friends, so kindly is their welcome, and so homelike and pleasant are the arrangements made for them. No one need be dull—something is always happening—a draper comes through with his pack of goods for sale; a farmer rides up with his daughters from a homestead thirty miles south, on their way to a dance held in a hall twenty miles further on; news too continually filters through—for the settlers all know one another, and take the keenest interest in each other's welfare. Catering is sometimes difficult. There are cows for milk, chickens and a kitchen garden, sheep too, in paddocks not far off; but all other provisions must either come in the weekly coach or by steamer to the small township of Okarito, seventeen miles away. Okarito is like other west coast harbours, in having a bar, which, in stormy weather, makes it impossible for even a small steamer to enter or leave the port. Often, for weeks at a time, the inhabitants of Waiho Gorge must depend on the mail coach for their supplies.

I had come back to learn more of the mountains and their ways, if only the weather would allow me to climb.

For a short expedition up the Franz Josef Glacier, a hut stocked with provisions and blankets stands ready a few hours' tramp from Waiho, and for a day on the Fox, the farmhouse at Weheka serves as base; but for any long climb up either glacier, the climber must be equipped with tent, sleeping-bag, food, clothes, and sometimes a small spirit-stove. The great drawback to such mountaineering is that these necessaries must all be carried, and, as my guide considered that I had enough to do to carry myself, my only share was my own small camera.

In Westland, an Alpine tent is made of thin white mackintosh, with mackintosh floor and loose outer fly, also of mackintosh. The tent measures six feet by seven feet. The ridge-pole is of rope slipped through the top of the tent, and fastened securely to the spikes of two ice-axes set up at each end. The rope is next made firm round heavy stones, and the strings of the fly are held in place by more stones. Sleeping-bags are of eider-down or of blankets doubled over and stitched. For food you have bread, butter, tinned meats, tinned fruit, tea and milk. I spent several nights in a tent and found it surprisingly comfortable. When the tent has to be pitched on bare rock, the floor, in spite of extra clothing and a sleeping-bag, makes a hard bed, especially if bad weather compels you to stay in the tent longer than one night; but if it is possible to camp near shrubs, you can then collect branches and ferns, and these, packed closely together under the mackintosh, make a floor like a spring mattress. Whichever it was—either soft or hard—I contrived to sleep very well.

My first long expedition from Waiho was up the Franz Josef Glacier to Cape Defiance Hut, with a climb next day up Mount Moltke, a mountain which rises immediately behind the hut and is between seven and eight thousand feet in height. It is an easy climb.

After an early breakfast we left the hut at half-past seven. First we climbed up a rough track through the bush, where coprosmas and currant-trees bore dense and gorgeous clusters of berries—red, yellow and pink; then over grassy slopes, and on and up, by rocky ridges and snowfields; again more rocks and more steep slopes of snow, until at eleven o'clock, we stood on the summit, with the pure air and the view for our reward.

On one side is the sea, to-day only partially seen through great masses of cloud floating below us. On the other side, all was clear, and before us stretched, from north to south, the whole range of the main Divide, from Elie de Beaumont to Mount Cook and beyond—a vision of whiteness on their background of blue sky.

While we watched, the distant peaks gradually disappeared behind white mist, and presently, as we climbed down the snow-slopes, we too were enveloped in mist, and walked as grey ghosts in a ghostly world. Before reaching Cape Defiance, the mist cleared, and out shone the sun once more.

From Waiho, the Franz Josef Glacier with its great white steps is a road ever beckoning onwards, and the ascent of Moltke is, so to speak, a halt by the way.

It was the end of April, and the Franz Josef was even more deeply crevassed than the Tasman had been a month before; the weather too was unsettled, with heavy clouds in the west—not fit weather in which to begin a long climb. After ten days of watching and waiting, the weather cleared. We, that is, the guide and I, left Waiho on a radiant afternoon, and climbed up to Cape Defiance Hut. Here we were welcomed enthusiastically by keas, young and old, who chattered on the bushes or hopped inside the hut.

ICE PINNACLES, ALMER GLACIER.

The following day was still fine, so after an early lunch, we set out to cross the glacier, the guide carrying our tent, food and change of clothing. At first the ice was smooth and easy to walk on, gradually the cracks grew deeper and the ridges narrower, and I had to be roped and to wait patiently while many steps were cut, and twice the guide left me sitting on the rucksack and went ahead to pick out the best route for us both to take. The glacier here is steep as well as broken, and you climb a thousand feet in a very short time.

We were by this time close to the side, opposite the Almer Glacier, a fine little glacier which fairly tumbles down the mountain side, ending in an extraordinary array of huge broken pinnacles, like so many Leaning Towers of Pisa—blocks of green and white ice, with summits half-melted and all ready to fall. We hurried quickly past, and, once on the mountain, were soon safe from danger of falling pinnacles or rolling boulder. A stiff climb of an hour took us up the ridge. First we climbed on loose shingle, then over rocks and slopes of slippery snow-grass; and, at about five thousand feet, we stood on the snow-line, among patches of snow, lying between big grey rocks. Even at this height, there were many roots of an Alpine ranunculus with leaves like those of an English buttercup, growing side by side with the edelweiss. The only bird was a tiny mountain wren with no tail, which fluttered about the rocks.

Our tent was pitched on the bare rock, and, with the help of a spirit "cooker," we had an excellent hot stew, followed by tinned apricots and many cups of tea.

At eight o'clock it began to rain, and rained or snowed quietly and continuously all night long. At dawn a thick mist hid glacier and mountains. We had hoped to climb up behind the Almer Glacier, and to ascend Mount Drummond, a mountain over eight thousand feet, which only one man, a surveyor, has ever climbed.

With the weather in its present mood, we could only wait where we were, and in the intervals of eating and sleeping, we whiled away the time in playing patience, with the cards set out on a towel on the floor.

It cleared a little in the afternoon, and we were able to crawl out and stretch our legs by scrambling up the rocks at the back of the tent. We felt cheered too, as we could again see the Franz Josef Glacier and dim outlines of the mountains.

After a chilly night, we had breakfast by candle-light at six o'clock. Later the sun rose in a cloudless, pale blue sky, showing snow lying in a thin covering close round our tent, and the tent fly coated with frozen sleet.

In spite of blue sky the weather still looked uncertain—not suitable for our intended attempt to climb Mount Drummond. We could only take advantage of the good weather while it lasted, and so we climbed higher up the snow-slopes of the rock on which we had camped, and over a steep ridge above the snow-slopes. From this point we had an excellent view of the head of the Franz Josef, and could see some four miles of its course curving downwards far beneath in a confused mass of broken ice—white shot with blue. The glacier is fed by an immense field of pure white snow, behind which rise several high peaks of the Alps. Directly opposite us was Graham's Saddle—a broad white stairway leading between two of the peaks, and affording access, as I knew, to the Tasman Glacier on the other side. Rocky spurs run out from the dividing range, and from another range at right angles, into this vast snowfield; and near the junction of the latter range with the Divide, Mount Spencer erects a steep, snowy cone of over 9,000 feet.

On our way back to camp, we stopped to look for quartz crystals, which form here in quantities, and stick out at all angles from the sides and overhanging portions of the rocks: most of them are clear as glass, six-sided and sharply pointed, some are an opaque green; they vary in size from an eighth of an inch to two or three inches, and are very hard to detach, even with the sharp point of an ice-axe.

As we rolled up the tent, the weather was clouding over, and no sooner were we well on the ice of the Franz Josef than snow began to fall, and continued falling until we reached Cape Defiance Hut.

It was not an enjoyable tramp down the glacier in the driving snow and on ice with a surface of polished glass—indeed it was one of those days that make you wonder whether it is worth while to climb at all. One old kea emphatically disapproved; he joined us, and perched on the ice near, and remonstrated loudly with us at our rashness in venturing on such a day; at last, we spoke so threateningly that he flew off in disgust.

We were soon soaked to the skin, as snow quickly finds its way through woollen jersey or tweed coat, and one cannot climb in a mackintosh. After six hours' incessant climbing, it was good to be safe inside the hut, and enjoy a fire, hot tea and dry blankets.

After the snowstorm came a high wind, which howled furiously round the hut that night. It was blowing still, when on the following afternoon we started on our final three hours' climb down the glacier; but it was sunny too, and the hot sun had slightly melted the ice, and made it less slippery, so that climbing was easier than on the previous day. As we came back along the forest track to Waiho Gorge, the wind dropped completely, and the close of the day could not have been more lovely. There, behind the forests, stood Mount Drummond, and its resplendent whiteness and inaccessibility seemed to mock us from afar.

The bad weather had made everyone in the valley anxious, fearing lest our tent might have been blown over or the glacier have proved impassable, and that morning two men had set forth towards the glacier as a search party, and had returned relieved, after seeing two black specks moving among the ice-falls.

Three weeks later we made another attempt to climb Mount Drummond.

All went well between Waiho and Cape Defiance; the glacier was in perfect condition, and you could walk anywhere without the least difficulty.

On the following day we crossed the glacier immediately below the hut, and were dismayed to find the surface more smoothly polished and glasslike than on the day when we came down from the Almer; we could not walk a yard without step-cutting, and we took two hours to climb three quarters of a mile. That brought us to the nearest point on the opposite side: to climb further would have been sheer waste of time. All we could do was to scramble a short way up the mountain side, and pitch the tent, hoping for better weather on the morrow. Alas for our hopes! The morning dawned dull and gloomy, with thick clouds rolling up from the sea, and by the time we had struck camp, down came the rain, and we had a wet and tedious climb back to Cape Defiance.

Rain poured in torrents all the next day, so we waited at the hut. The next day again was equally wet; however, at breakfast we finished our last crumbs of bread and biscuit, and were compelled to go, however bad the weather.

The keas had entertained us during our stay at Cape Defiance by their absurd cries and friendly inquisitiveness, and a whole troop of them escorted us some way down the glacier, until finding our progress very slow, they flew away to shelter.

We were absent so long, that when in the afternoon we walked calmly into the hotel, we found that a search party was intending to start with lanterns at five o'clock next morning to look for us.

On the Fox Glacier we had fewer adventures, and were more successful in carrying through what we attempted, though there too we were compelled to strike camp in the rain and trudge back to the homestead, drenched to the skin and with our mountain unclimbed.

At last came a bright sunny morning, free from any threatening cloud-bank out to sea. We set off hopefully on horseback and rode three miles through the bush to the foot of the glacier. We left the horses to feed along the track, then climbed for three hours up the glacier. Next we lighted a fire among the stones, in a sheltered nook under the steep mountain side, and had lunch and a short spell.

Above its first smooth layers of ice the Fox is tremendously broken into gigantic pinnacles, impossible for climbing, and you are forced to take refuge amongst boulders and slippery rocks at the side. Higher still is the main ice-fall of the Fox—more pinnacles and ridges of ice coming down between the mountains in a wide frozen cascade—almost as magnificent as the great ice-fall on the Franz Josef. We crossed the glacier at the foot of the fall and did not attempt to climb up far among the séracs, but made for the side, and wormed our way up steep gullies through coarse wet grass, and then scrambled along smooth, glacier-worn rocks high above, where we held on carefully to flax, cotton-grass, or any overhanging branch.

Late in the afternoon we came out on the bed of a precipitous creek, and on the further side of it found a small platform, some ten feet by seven, thickly overgrown with rank green grass, open to the glacier on one side, and on the others ringed about closely with many trees. Here we pitched the tent, with a soft floor of ferns and the leafy branches of veronicas, senecios and broadleaf trees. A fireplace of stones was soon built against the mountain side among ferns and biddies, and the wood fire burnt cheerily: it was too cold for sitting outside, so we had dinner inside the tent, looking out at our camp-fire and the dark cliff beyond the noisy creek; later the moon rose, showing the glacier beneath, white in the moonlight.

At 9 p.m. we crawled into our sleeping-bags and slept. We awoke cold during the night, but after warming the tent with a small spirit lamp, we ate slices of currant loaf, and soon went to sleep again. At four-thirty the camp fire was lighted, and at five o'clock we had breakfast. It was an excellent breakfast of tea, bread and butter and delicious nectarine jam, and I even had a boiled egg.

MOUNT MOLTKE AND VICTORIA GLACIER
FROM CHANCELLOR RIDGE.

At seven we left our camp and set off up the creek-bed for the summit of Chancellor Ridge. The dawn was clear and cold, with the glacier and forests in cold grey shadow; the sea was a quiet grey, and above the horizon we saw the shadow of the earth in deep blue-grey on a sky of orange. Striking away from the creek across slopes of snow grass, we climbed up rocky ridges, and at about five thousand feet came out on a bare ridge, where I was put on the rope: then on up a steep snowfield, and over a rounded dome of snow where the surface was like pie-crust; next over slippery ice which had a sprinkling of snow, and where steps had to be chipped. Finally we had a stiff climb up the actual summit—a short and steep knob of rock, half concealed by snow; and on the top we found a tiny ledge of grey rock, with streaks of white and green quartz, and scanty green moss clinging to it. The summit is only between seven and eight thousand feet high, in New Zealand hardly to be considered a mountain, still, when we gained it successfully, my guide said briefly: "First lady to reach the summit, I must congratulate you." So we shook hands and were happy.

It was now ten o'clock and brilliantly sunny, and we stood alone in a world of snow. Below lay the head of the Fox Glacier—a great snowfield encircled by mountains. Immediately above the head of the glacier stood Mount Tasman, only a couple of miles from us, its base firmly planted in the snow, from base to summit clothed in a spotless mantle of pure white. On the far side of the range bounding the Fox, was Mount Cook: as seen from this point, a snow mountain of one aspiring peak. To the left of Tasman stretched a succession of snow-clad mountains, continuing until joined by another range at right-angles. Rising in a mountain at the head of the latter range, was the Victoria Glacier—a long river of dirty white ice, flowing down towards the Fox in a deep valley on the left of Chancellor Ridge.

The main direction of the Southern Alps is parallel with the coastline, and when we turned our backs upon Mount Tasman we looked across the Victoria Glacier to a dazzling snow peak beyond, and down the Fox valley with its forest ranges to boundless miles of blue sea. On the sea—apparently floating on its surface—were narrow strips of cloud—grey, white and gold—and on the shore, some twenty miles distant, we saw lines of white surf on the irregular beaches between the tree-clad bluffs.

After a well-earned lunch of sardines, sandwiches and pineapple, we retraced our steps down the slopes of snow to the rocky ridge, and from there took a different route and climbed down a steep rock-face. It was not very easy climbing, as the ground, sheltered from the sun, was still frozen hard; so my guide kept a cautious hand on the rope, while I found foothold and handhold. Below the rock-face we came back to snow grass and stony creeks, and so to last night's camping ground.

At half-past two we left the camp for the climb down. While we were still on the glacier, the sun set in a sky of deep red, changing to orange, yellow and pale blue. Ice-steps are hard to see in the short New Zealand dusk, and by the time we reached the final moraine it was quite dark, and we congratulated ourselves on being safely off the ice. No horses were to be found, so we had to walk for the last three miles through the bush, and at half-past seven walked quietly into the farmhouse sitting-room, tired but triumphant.

For a final view of the mountains, nothing can be better than a ride down the Waiho river-bed to the coast. The Waiho is a short river of thirteen miles, flowing in a river-bed three-quarters of a mile wide. It flows always as a roaring torrent, sometimes a narrow blue stream through the grey stones, but in flood-time a mighty river of yellow water churning madly between its banks, and whirling along with it lumps of ice, stones and mighty forest trees. By the river banks and on rocky islands in its bed are many low-growing shrubs, most of them some variety of coprosma—"black scrub" as the settlers call it—which may either creep along the ground or grow to a height of ten feet; and in the autumn every bush, large and small, was laden with berries—berries of black, crimson, scarlet, orange, white, grey or blue. Many of the berries are translucent, and shine in the sunlight like beads of Venetian glass, and the trees are blue or red from top to bottom with only slight suggestions of green leaf and black twig. In New Zealand the mistletoe berry is yellow, and was particularly abundant this autumn, growing on any tree, among branches already lavishly gay. Above the river banks tall currant-trees bear clusters of pink, white or black berries, while the pines have berries of red or purple. Often too, hanging from the branches of the trees, and twining round the ferns and drooping grey-green "gie-gies" which clothe their trunks, are garlands of scarlet supple-jack.

With the Waiho at its normal level, one can ride close to the water, and the horses will pick their way carefully among the boulders and fallen tree-trunks, cantering on any smooth stretch of grass. While the horse chooses the way, his rider is free to give full attention to the beauty of river, mountain and forest.

Looking back from the mouth of the river we saw the whole range of the Alps. In the centre of the picture was the Franz Josef Glacier with its immense white snowfield behind, and the Almer Glacier flowing into it on the left: prominent above the snowfield stood Mount Spencer in raiment of white, like a stately lady proud of her position: stretching away from Mount Spencer and the Franz Josef Glacier on either side, as far as eye could see, peak after peak was outlined in delicate purity against the blue, the summits varying in height and shape, some broad and rounded, others sharp and pointed, no peak standing out unduly from the rest—a range of mountains absolutely right in proportion, one harmonious whole, and all beautiful together. As seen from here, the Alps have as foreground forest-clad mountains encircling the Franz Josef Glacier and rising one behind the other below the snowy peaks; gradually they give place to quite low hills and to the scrub of the river-bed on which our horses stood.

As we rode on towards the sea, we passed clear pools left by the river in the shingle, and in the still water the mountains were reflected; we saw Mount Cook, Tasman and the rest at our very feet, while in reality they were at a distance of forty miles and more.

To-day all was calm, but the Waiho in its short course of thirteen miles can be cruel and terrible, and only lately a man was drowned as he tried to cross it. Lying in the river-bed are the gaunt bleached corpses of forest-trees, a few all the way and very many at the mouth, where they lie thickly along the shore; these trees had their roots undermined by the Waiho in flood-time, and when the flood went down the trees fell and died—they were the one sad sight of an otherwise perfect morning.

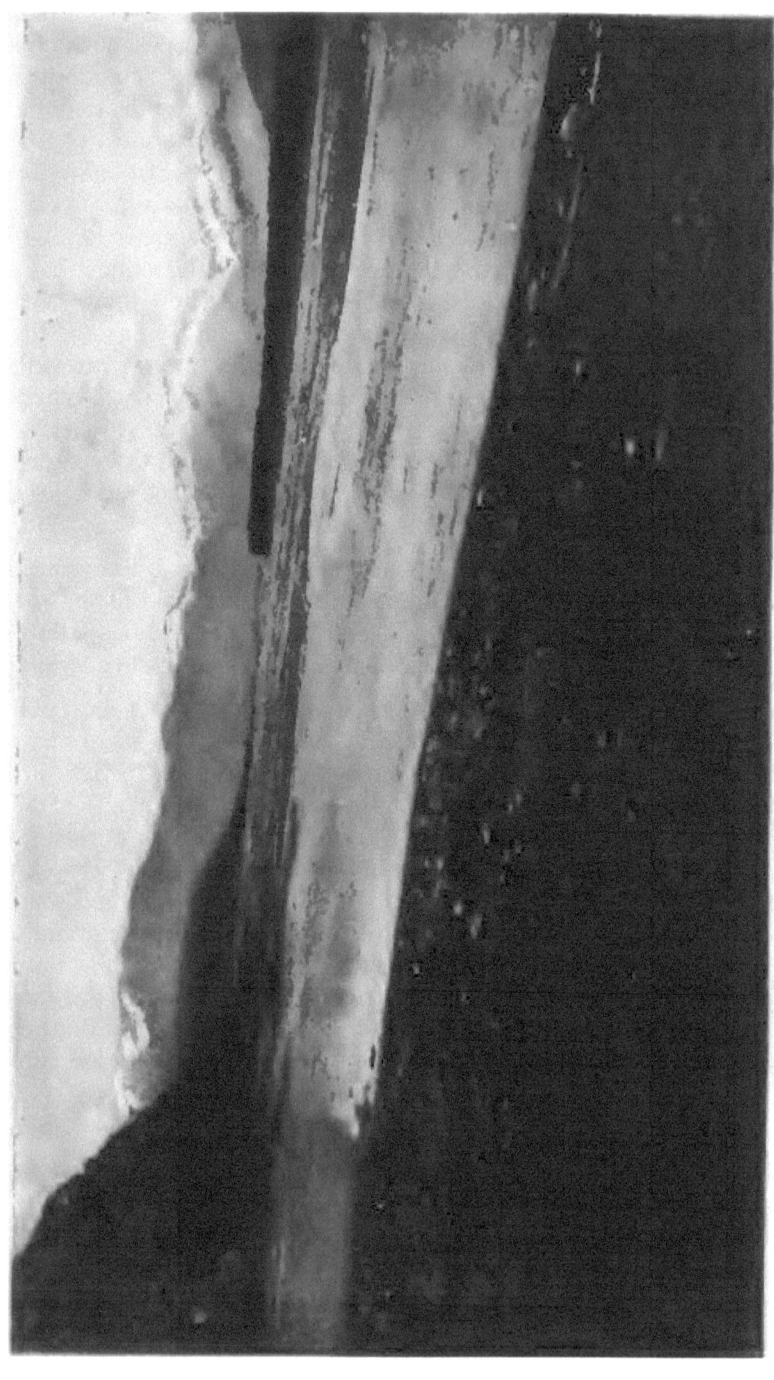

SOUTHERN ALPS FROM MOUTH OF WAIHO RIVER.

After rounding a steep bush-clad bluff, we came out on the shore of the Tasman Sea, a quiet grey and blue sea, with the tide coming in, and great white curling breakers dashing against the beach—those mighty breakers which are ever rolling on the Pacific coasts—we cantered through the surf on firm grey sand, the spray flying round us as we rode. Ever in the distance, against the blue, rose the snowy peaks, whose loveliness compelled us to look again and yet again, until it was a relief to rest the eyes on the grey sameness of the sand.

Forty years ago this beach was thronged with miners seeking gold; now not one lives here, and there is very little gold left, though we did come across three "beach combers," who were washing sand in wooden troughs, in the hope of finding a deposit of gold at the bottom.

The bluffs, which here run down to the sea, are ancient glacial moraines—high-piled heaps of boulders and loose soil, covered now with wind-swept tea-tree bushes, tall forest trees and crimson rata vine, and between the headlands, where once the glaciers flowed, are peaceful lagoons bordered with flax plants and rushes.

At low tide you may skirt the bluffs on the sand between sea and cliff, but sometimes you must ride over them—up a steep track through scrub and forest, where a horse accustomed to the beach will carry you safely; and from his back, you look down through tall brown trunks on the blue sea far below.

A ride of six miles from the mouth of the Waiho brings you to Okarito—a tiny township and port—its one street all grass-grown, and only a few houses and the wharf to mark what was, in the days of gold, a big and thriving town. In those days it had two Churches, many banks and hotels, and in the saloons, gay doings night after night.

Another eight mile ride through the forest brought us to a small hotel, where I joined the mail coach which took me back to trains and towns, and very sorrowfully I said goodbye to the mountains and to my friends in Westland.

CHAPTER XIII
THE WAITOMO CAVES

As in other countries, so in New Zealand, there are limestone caves, with stalactites and stalagmites, and all their effect of wonder and mystery. They are found in some of the low hills which rise in the heart of the Maori-owned "King Country," and as they are only a few miles from the Main Trunk railway line, which connects Wellington with Auckland, they can be very conveniently visited by tourists going north or south.

The distance from Wellington to the caves is three hundred miles. Even on the main lines the average speed of an express train is only twenty-five miles an hour, so that a journey of three hundred miles takes a whole day, and gives the traveller many excellent opportunities for studying the landscape.

The trains run on a 3 foot 10 inch gauge; except for a few miles in the South Island, there is but a single line throughout the Dominion; often the trains accomplish well-nigh impossible feats in crawling up and down precipitous gorges, and yet so carefully are they handled that an accident is almost an unheard-of occurrence. Nearly all the first-class carriages are on the corridor plan, with a gangway up the middle. There are two seats on one side and only one on the other, and the seats have movable backs, made to face either way. The seats are numbered and can be reserved separately.

The second-class cars have straight rows of cushioned seats set lengthwise along the sides of the train and are not very comfortable; the fares on them are the same as the English third-class fares, while the first-class fare is always half as much again. There is never any difficulty about food on a long journey. The express trains have restaurant cars and provide excellent meals, charging only 2s. for early dinner or late tea. If you happen to be on a train that has no restaurant car, the train considerately stops at suitable hours for lunch or tea, and you find everything ready, either at the station refreshment room or in a hotel close by, and are warned, at the end of your meal, by a loudly-rung handbell, that the train is ready to go on again.

Neither is there the least difficulty with luggage. The check system is in vogue. On showing your ticket, each box is labelled and numbered, duplicates of the numbers are given to the passenger, and the New Zealand Government assumes full responsibility for the luggage. On a through ticket from Wellington to Auckland, the traveller may, after the first thirty miles, break his journey as often as he pleases, and, if he takes two days or a month on the road, will find his belongings safely stored in the Auckland Left Luggage Office.

On leaving Wellington, the railway skirts the west coast, and runs through rocky country, gracefully covered with native trees, chiefly manuka and kowhai: I was there in winter, too soon to see the yellow fringes of kowhai bloom, which in September are

> "Flung for gift on Taupo's face,
> Sign that Spring is come."

The kowhai is one of the prettiest trees, with feathery green leaves and laburnum-like flowers, and shares with the fuchsia and the ribbon-wood the distinction of losing its leaves in the winter, and standing, though only for a short time, with bare branches. The views are fine on either side. On the west you look out on the ocean and a succession of irregular bays, whose high cliffs rise steeply up from the water: some miles away to the east, stand ranges of snow-capped mountains, remote and beautiful, with white clouds floating between the peaks.

Between the mountains and the sea is level ground, excellent for grazing and dairying, and settlements and towns are rapidly growing. To the north of the plains is a rough country of swamp alternating with low, rounded hills. This land has been partly cleared and the beginning of settlements made, grass is sown in places and cabbage trees are left standing in the paddocks. Beyond, come stretches of fern and scrub—bracken and tea-tree repeated indefinitely for many miles—until presently the line runs through vast forests—thousands of acres of big bush—pines, ratas and the rest, with all their glorious entanglement of creepers and ferns.

Later, while the train still runs through the forests, passengers wrap themselves in their rugs and try to sleep. It is not a very successful attempt, as at each stop you are roused—sometimes by the entrance of fresh passengers, and always by the guard who comes round to demand tickets.

At midnight I reached my stopping-place, found a hotel and a bed, and slept comfortably.

Next morning I was up at 7, and after a good breakfast of fried egg and bacon—the customary fare in country hotels—went on again by train for another fifty miles. At 11 o'clock I reached Hangatiki, a solitary little station, near a hotel and a few small houses. Here a coach with three horses was waiting, to drive the remaining six miles to the Waitomo Caves. The scenery was very much the same as before—small hills and swamp-land, with scrub of fern and manuka, varied by great patches of tall forest-trees.

The whole of this district, the so-called "King Country," forms a Maori Kingdom in the centre of the North Island, and is, with the exception of some few holdings, in Maori hands. This land was formally assured to Maori chiefs, after one of the wars between English and Maoris, fifty years ago, and though the Maoris rejoice in its possession, they yet make little use of it. English settlers, who would turn it to good account find it difficult to buy; as, even if one Maori is willing to sell, he cannot sell without the consent of all the other Maoris, who, in common with himself, have rights of possession over any particular section.

At Waitomo I found a government hostel, a very imposing two-storied wooden building, lighted by electricity, and with hot and cold water laid on in every bedroom.

I was the only tourist, and when I asked the manager if a guide could show me one of the caves after dinner that evening, he expressed great regret that a party of visitors, whom he expected from Rotorua, had not arrived. However, as I was quite certain that I wished to see the caves, even if unattended, he finally summoned the guide, and sent one of the maids from the hotel with me as chaperone.

It is no light matter to visit these caves. Having found guide and chaperone, the tourist is next expected to hire a suitable outfit, and to don nailed boots of strong leather, also a tunic and baggy knickers made of blue and white striped galatea, and is finally provided with an oil lantern, while the guide carries a lighted candle and a reel of magnesium wire.

The guide proved to be a boy of good education, who had come out from Home in search of adventure, he had worked for a time in a solicitor's office in Wellington, and was doing a little guiding by way of variety.

It was a pitch-black night and we were glad of our lanterns. The entrance to the first cave is a quarter of a mile away from the hotel and is approached by a rough and muddy track. You enter the cave through a rocky archway among the bush. This cave was first shown to white men in 1886, though the Maoris knew of it many years ago and avoided it and all such places as the abodes of evil spirits.

The Waitomo Cave consists of a vast series of limestone caverns, with endless stalactites hanging from the roofs, and pure white columns rising to meet them from the floor. There is very little bare rock, wherever you look are limestone formations, richly covering the surface and assuming beautiful or most fantastic shapes. One great cluster of columns is like the pipes of an organ; in one cavern you have a poulterer's store, with geese and turkeys, heads downwards, hanging from the ceiling; in another is a greengrocer's shop, with great carrots and parsnips of yellow or creamy limestone; on the floor are many beginnings of stalagmites, formed by the overhead drippings, and which the iron in the water has coloured yellow or brown—these are poached eggs or Stewart Island oysters, according to fancy. In one grotto hangs a beautiful white shawl—the Waitomo Blanket—it hangs in graceful folds, and the iron has given it a broad brown border. All these caves are entirely untouched and unspoilt, they have not been in any way altered or improved, not even by the introduction of electric light. As we went slowly through, the guide kept lighting fresh lengths of magnesium wire, which softly and delightfully illuminated each fresh marvel. In one place he made a veritable bonfire of the wire, and displayed a lofty hall, very white and glittering, ornamented with lovely white pendants of all shapes and sizes.

An underground river flows through the caves: when you reach the last cavern, the lights of candle and lantern are extinguished, and in perfect silence and almost total darkness you enter a small boat, which the guide pulls gently along on a wire rope fixed to the wall; then you are told to look up, and there on the roof are myriads of tiny glow-worms, by whose light huge stalactites are visible. The cavern continues for some two hundred yards, with a very uneven roof, all craggy projections of rock and limestone, and in every nook and corner, like stars in the sky, shine glow-worm lamps of varying intensity, giving just light enough to show the outlines of this mysterious place, and in the black water roof and glow-worms are dimly reflected.

Next morning I again put on Government boots and cave dress, and, mounted astride on a good horse, went with the guide and a friend of his—a boy from the Waitomo Store—for a short ride of between two and three miles to see two more caves. Both of these were entered by low openings among the trees of a bush-covered hill.

The larger of the two has a succession of long narrow passages, connecting several lofty halls, and the walls of passages and grottoes alike are covered with deposits of lime, much of it looking as though incrustations of brown coral had been thickly spread over every square inch of surface. Here too are glittering hanging shapes and many strange formations, some reminding you of huge cauliflowers, others of birds' heads.

A narrow stream flows through, and, on the "ghost walk"—most appropriately named—you hear an uncanny noise, caused innocently enough by a waterfall which rushes down the rocks outside.

The last cave is the smallest, and, except that it has no glow-worm cavern, the most beautiful of the three Waitomo Caves. Each and all of the caverns and passages which compose it are equally lovely, from floor to roof one gorgeous adornment of pure white crystal, which shines in countless jewelled forms in the glow of the light from the magnesium wire. One hall was particularly beautiful with multitudes of hanging stalactites; another was crowded with slender pillars stretching away into the darkness. In some caverns are small white figures perched on rocky ledges—one set like chessmen on a board; from the roofs of the caverns hang several thin white shawls with hem-stitched edges, while innumerable snowy pendants taper elegantly downwards to meet white columns rising from the floor. The whole effect of this wondrous cave is of some magician's palace of fairyland, built for Oberon and Titania, and to be gazed at in reverent amazement by mortal eyes.

Apart from the caves, there is little to detain the traveller at Waitomo. There are few settlements and fewer tracks among the surrounding swamps and forests. I climbed a low hill which has been partially cleared. From the top I looked down upon a very new homestead of wood, its paddocks partly cleared and all fenced in with barbed wire. All round me on every side stretched ridges behind ridges of low hills clothed with sombre forests: while forty miles away, bounding the view to the south, were the snowy peaks of volcanic mountains, one of them over eight thousand feet high.

CHAPTER XIV

NEW ZEALAND'S WONDERLAND

In the middle of the North Island of New Zealand is a marvellous district, stretching from White Island, in the Bay of Plenty, to the active volcano of Ngaruhoe, a hundred and fifty miles to the south, and varying in breadth from ten to twenty miles. Throughout the whole of this area no one knows what will happen next. Strange underground rumblings are heard; earthquake shocks are felt; in places the whole countryside is puffing out volumes of steam; and only twenty-seven years ago, a mountain, believed for centuries to be quite harmless, suddenly burst into violent eruption, and destroyed three villages with over a hundred Maoris and several Europeans. It is all very interesting: but as one man who lives close to a boiling lake explained to me, you can hardly enjoy living there, because you are always close to forces that no one really understands.

For the tourist the centre from which to see all the wonders is Rotorua—a very new town of straight streets at right angles to one another. The houses are of wood, roofed with corrugated iron: it is hardly safe to build with any other material in Rotorua, as two feet below the surface you are always liable to come upon a spring of hot water.

The town is owned by the Government, which has built and maintains a hospital and sanatorium and fine bath-houses, surrounded by extensive and well laid-out grounds. In the grounds are planted many firs and gums and tall Australian wattles. When I saw them, the early-flowering wattles were a glory of golden blossom and delicate green leaves under the bright blue sky of a New Zealand winter. There are flower-beds with daffodils and other bulbs, rose-trees, and all the flowers of an English garden; also good tennis lawns and bowling-greens, and both town and gardens are set by the shores of a big shining lake. Round the lake are low, rather bare green hills, and on one side a mountain of two thousand feet.

The first thing about Rotorua that strikes the visitor as strange is the smell of sulphur, which greets you even before the train stops at the railway station, and which you never lose while you remain in the place. When you walk out to see the town, your second surprise is the steam. It is not actually in the streets; but less than two miles away, behind a long avenue of gum-trees, you see masses of steam constantly rising in larger or smaller columns, and by the lake and away on the opposite side, more puffs of steam. The steam comes from hot springs and hot rivulets, which you find side by side with streams of cold water, from pools of boiling mud, and from fascinating geysers.

LAKE ROTORUA.

A regular cluster of all these marvels is to be seen beyond the gum-trees, at Whaka, in a few acres of rocky white ground, overgrown with thickets of stunted "manuka" scrub, with its tiny evergreen leaves and rough brown stem. There is a large Maori settlement here, and another close to the cold water of Rotorua Lake, among more boiling pools and springs.

The Maoris have always loved the hot water, and Maori villages have existed here long before Europeans thought of making a town and using Rotorua as a health resort. The Maoris use the hot pools to bathe in, and the Maori women wash their clothes in the hot streams, rubbing the things with soap on a convenient stone, and then boiling them in a still hotter stream close at hand. They even use the springs for cooking. They fix a wooden box over a steaming patch of soil; inside the box they place the kettle or the pot filled with meat and vegetables, cover the whole with coarse sacking and leave the food to simmer.

As you walk about these strange places, the ground, sprinkled with sulphur, alum, red or yellow ochre, is hot under your feet. At Whaka you unexpectedly come upon deep holes where dark grey mud is always boiling. In one corner is a large pool of oily mud boiling perpetually in circles, and as it boils, the mud goes leaping up into the air like a company of frogs. There are many geysers here, but they are less active than formerly, and the most wonderful—which, with the help of bars of soap thrown down its throat, used to play always in honour of any royal personage—has not played for several years.

How am I to describe a geyser? You walk on hot ground up to a low mound of white rock with a round hole in the middle of it. You look into the hole, and see, far below, bubbling water, with steam rising from it—very innocent apparently. Presently you are warned to stand back, and up comes the hot water, rushing through the geyser's throat, straight at first, then sloping outwards, and rising to any height from two feet to a hundred, in a beautiful spreading column of sparkling drops, curving over at the top like an ostrich feather; and round the water and above it steam rises in clouds. Some geysers play with absolute regularity, every four minutes or every half hour or at some other fixed time; others are more capricious, and play only once or twice a day, and at quite irregular intervals. I waited a whole afternoon hoping that the best of the Whaka geysers would play, and in the end it did, and up gushed the hot water to a height of forty feet or so—a magnificent display of sparkling diamonds. Most of these hot waters contain sulphur and other minerals, and bathing in them is an excellent cure for rheumatism, skin complaints and other ailments. In Rotorua you can even have a delightful bath of liquid mud, which is like grey cream mixed with oil, and makes one's skin feel as soft as silk.

The railroad ends at Rotorua. Beyond, you must either drive in coach or motor, ride on horseback, or go in a steam launch across the lake.

The country round is singularly desolate and almost uninhabited. Mile after mile the roads run between low hills covered with bracken and manuka scrub, with here and there some scanty tussock grass. Many thousands of pines, larches, gums and birches have been planted by prisoners who are kept in camps among the hills, and more trees are being planted all the time and are growing well; so, in a few years, the countryside will look less dreary.

Among the low undulating hills other solitary hills stand out, of strange forbidding shape, either flat-topped ridges or cones—most of them extinct volcanoes, or not quite extinct even now: as from some of them puffs of steam are always rising, not from the tops of the hills, but from cracks on the hillsides. In some places the scattered puffs are concentrated in great blowholes: you hear a mighty roar inside the hill, and from a narrow throat-hole a gigantic mass of steam comes pouring out perpetually—the safety-valve of some internal machine.

At Waimangu, seventeen miles from Rotorua, I was shown the spot where two girls and a man were all killed by a geyser a few years ago. The girls had been warned not to go too close, but they were anxious to take photographs and disregarded the warning. The guide sprang forward to pull them back, when suddenly up spouted the geyser to the extraordinary height of fifteen hundred feet, and the boiling water dashed down upon them all and carried them away and killed them in an instant. Since that tragedy the geyser has not played again, but a blowhole close by is beginning to send out jets of water as well as steam, and may in time develop into a geyser.

Waimangu is only a few miles from Tarawera Mountain, which in June, 1886, burst into eruption, and covered everything within a radius of eight miles with a deep deposit of grey mud, and scattered thin layers of mud and ashes to a much greater distance. After the eruption, a very heavy rain fell and wore deep channels in all directions through the mud. In consequence, round Waimangu and the adjoining lake of Rotomahana you see the strangest, most desolate scenery of grey gullies, by this time scantily sprinkled with bracken and "toi-toi" grass, a tall, white-flowering grass like pampas grass. Waimangu itself is principally a valley of steam, sulphur, boiling mud, and little mud volcanoes. On the ground are deposits of sulphur and alum, and you walk cautiously on patches of hot, dry ground. Among the hot mud and through it all runs a hot stream, with some variety of green algæ growing in it. The hot stream flows into Rotomahana Lake, where once the famous pink and white terraces were to be seen. they were destroyed by the Tarawera eruption. Still the lake is sufficiently wonderful: a lake of chalky blue water, actually boiling at one end and cold at the other, lying in a crater, with the high, oblong-shaped mass of Tarawera Mountain on one side. A great gap in the side of the mountain is plainly visible, reminding all who see it of the hidden forces ever at work.

On the other side of a low ridge, half a mile away, is Tarawera Lake, several miles across—a lake of quite ordinary, clear, cold water. The hills surrounding it are partly covered with bush, and among the living trees still stand the skeletons of trees destroyed by the eruption.

A few miles from Waimangu is another valley, and in it a succession of primrose-coloured terraces, which are gradually being formed of silica left by the overflow of a lake of boiling sulphur, and very pretty they are. A lake of yellowish green water lies above several long shallow steps of pale primrose silica; all around are clumps of manuka and patches of brilliantly green mosses; and looking across the terraces, you see mile beyond mile of level plain, all a study in browns, with a dim blue ridge of hill on the distant horizon.

Each of these wonder-spots has some special characteristic which distinguishes it from the others. The valley of the primrose terraces was one of sulphur—fringes of yellow sulphur floating round the edges of hot green lakes and pools; sulphur surrounding hot steam-holes; sulphur colouring the rocks and lying thickly upon the ground. In another place, where, again I saw sulphur, alum and hot springs, the chief wonder was the boiling mud: horrible, deep pools of dark grey mud and petroleum, always working away and heaving themselves up and down like the huge cauldrons of wicked witches.

Fifty miles south of Rotorua is Weirakei. Here you see a marvellous valley, which not only has excellent examples of all the strange sights of this wonderland, but is also exceedingly pretty. It is a narrow valley, on either side are high cliffs of grey rock streaked with pink. At the bottom, among dainty ferns and bright green moss and silvery lichen runs a brawling stream of clear, cold, blue water. Beside the stream, and up the cliff sides, grow quantities of manuka, with feathery green sprays; and other shrubs, with tiny green leaves and small white berries: and on every hand, puffs of steam rise and float away over the greenery.

This valley is specially noted for geysers, which play in absolute regularity one after another in beautiful columns of glittering water-drops, the columns varying in height from ten to forty feet. One geyser shoots out from a truly awesome opening, in shape like a dragon's mouth, formed in a mass of old-rose coloured silica, and torrents of boiling water pour out of the mouth and down a steep slope of more pink silica, and you stand on hot rock at the bottom of the slope, watching the water come right up to your feet. Below the geyser is another wonder—a small pool, deep blue in colour, and from its depths some gas is continually rising to the surface, like a flash of dazzling lightning. This is a valley of many colours; the deposits of silica are of white, pink, or emerald-green—there are mud-pools of cream or pink, where the boiling mud rises up and falls over in shapes resembling roses or lilies: and always the setting is of green, leafy sprays, emerald mosses and luxuriant ferns.

Near Weirakei is another valley, where the stream which flows through it is a boiling creek, fed by tiny tributary streams of boiling water, all of chalky white. Half-way up this valley is a wide waterfall of boiling water tumbling over salmon-coloured cliffs; and all about, watered by the hot spray, grow lovely ferns and feathery manuka. There are three little pools in a cluster, two quite hot and one cold, their margins only a foot apart. You see a large lake of hot blue water, and on its surface is a floating scum like oily soapsuds. There are twin lakelets of brilliant blue. Deep down in a hollow is a lake of deep rose-colour. Side by side are lakelets, one of deep blue, the other of emerald green. You are shown a large mud volcano. Near it is a deep hole of fathomless black water. At the entrance of the valley is a big lake of hot blue water, surrounded by high grey cliffs. Here and throughout the thermal district, it is wise to follow the guide warily among the scrub and on the hot rock, for outside the track are holes and swamps; and if you once slip, you may get a scald from which you will never recover.

Six miles beyond Weirakei is Taupo Lake, a great lake, twenty-five miles long. On the right of it are dim grey hills; and opposite them high cliffs of grey, streaked with pink and white. Beyond the far end of the lake, on a clear day, are to be seen snow-covered mountains, one of them a still active volcano, with smoke pouring out from its snowy crater.

To the east of Rotorua, between that town and the Bay of Plenty, is still volcanic country, but the strange sights grow gradually less frequent. You see occasional puffs of steam among the bracken, and are told of hot springs where refreshing baths may be taken, but it is all a more normal country of lake, forest and swampland.

A coach road, principally composed of yellow sand—as stone is scarce or almost unobtainable—runs from Rotorua to the Bay, a distance of eighty miles, and a very good road it is in dry weather. It runs past lakes surrounded by untouched bush, through the heart of sombre forests, and up and down steep gorges, where you see magnificent tree-ferns, "nikau" palms and many giant trees. The North Island forest is different from that in the South Island, though some of the trees are the same. There are still rimus and other pines, but the feathery beeches of the south are less frequent. The trees in the north are on the whole more massive and gloomy: there are great "tawas" and honeysuckles, with enormous trunks and dark glossy leaves; also many great ratas and totaras. The supple-jack erects its slender black stems among the tall trees, and the bush-lawyer drapes fuchsias and tree-ferns with festoons of green; but it is all far less luxuriant than the Westland bush. There are fewer ferns and mosses, often you see patches of bare brown earth among bare tree-trunks, and, scattered frequently through this northern forest, are the bleached branches of dead or dying trees.

Some twenty miles from the sea, the hills, which in this part of New Zealand run down to the coast in long parallel ridges, stand back on either side, and the country opens out into a great plain—eighty thousand acres of swamp-land. This will one day be some of the most fertile land in the district. It is now being drained by a steam dredge, which forces its way straight through the swamp, leaving a wide dyke of dark brown water. At the beginning of the swamp there is a wide river, to be crossed only by a flat-bottomed punt, worked on a steel cable. The passengers sit still and the horses are driven on to the boat, and the current quickly pushes the boat to the opposite side.

Later, the road runs along the coast, and reaches an inlet from the ocean of, perhaps, a mile wide. The water has to be crossed in a little ferry boat, worked by oil and petrol. The horses are quite used to it and go up the hanging gangway willingly enough; but sometimes, when the sea is rough, it is not safe to venture, and passengers must wait for several hours on an inhospitable, sandy shore.

All this part of the country through which the coach runs, from Rotorua to Opotiki, on the Bay of Plenty, is some of the most isolated in New Zealand. Inland are scattered Maori settlements, and tiny English townships by the coast. During the last few years the land away back has been, to a great extent, taken up—forests are being cut down and swamps drained—and in a few years' time, the east coast will be one of the chief centres for sheep runs and dairy farms.

On the Bay of Plenty, settlers tell you of cows and sheep, the price of wool and the prospects of new cheese factories. In spite of that you are still in "Uncanny Country," for there, forty miles out to sea, is the cone of White Island, which was once an active volcano. Its activities are now reduced to a large blowhole and a lake of ever-boiling sulphur, from both of which by day and night pour forth volumes of steam, and sometimes the north wind carries the smell of sulphur to you across the bay.

CHAPTER XV
AUCKLAND

The people of Auckland love to think of their city as "last, loneliest, loveliest, exquisite, apart," and when they are away from it, they miss its sunny climate, with the glint of the sunlight on the water and through the water of its spacious harbours. It is the largest town in New Zealand, and has a population of one hundred and ten thousand inhabitants. It is situated on a neck of land, at its narrowest only eight miles wide, with the shining sea on both sides; and it is to its position that Auckland owes its unique and elusive charm. There are two harbours—one on the east, the other on the west, and at the eastern harbour wharves are built; here big ships lie at anchor close to the main streets of the city, and an excellent service of trams connects the wharves with shops and hotels and distant suburbs.

When in 1840, New Zealand was declared a British colony, it was decided to make Auckland the capital, and so it remained until 1864, when the seat of Government was transferred to Wellington, as being more central for the whole country.

The site of Auckland itself as well as the country round it is all volcanic, and in every direction are small cone-shaped, grass-covered hills, each just high enough for a pleasant afternoon's walk. From any one of their summits you look down on an innocent crater at your feet; on the hillside sheep browse and citizens play golf; and beyond, on a clear day, Auckland lies spread out before you—its streets and harbours, with sea and islands and distant forest ranges. The eastern harbour has no definite entrance, so numerous are the inlets and islands which you see on all sides; but bush-covered Rangitoto Island—a large extinct volcanic cone—forms a wall of several miles to the inner harbour; and for the outer harbour you may look across the Hauraki Gulf to Great Barrier Island, sixty miles away—a fine expanse of water for yachting and all kinds of boating.

Auckland is truly a garden city. A deep, green gully, rich in beautiful tree-ferns and other native plants, runs through the centre, spanned by a wide and elegant bridge of iron and white stone; in the middle of the town are delightful public gardens with trees, green grass and gay flower-beds; private houses close to the shops have gardens in which grow violets and great camellia bushes, laden in winter with pink or white blossoms; tall white arum lilies run riot wherever they can find standing room; while close to the harbour are survivals of the ancient forest—big, gnarled Christmas trees, in summer a mass of crimson bloom. Just outside the chief thoroughfare is the Domain—a hundred acres of park-land with grass and groups of trees—the inalienable property of all the citizens. The town and suburbs are scattered over several miles. There are groups of houses beside the Domain; others encircling the green conical hills; and often the houses are built near some arm of the harbour, separated from it by trees and grass and a steep cliff, with always wide open views of sea and tree-clad islands.

MAORI ANCESTRAL FIGURE.

Even more delightful than its natural beauties is the fact that Auckland has no slums. There are a few narrow streets and mean houses, but the overcrowding and dirt of the poorer quarters of an English town do not exist, and the Auckland city authorities have firmly resolved that they never shall. There is plenty of space, so the houses need not be built too close together, and very few of them are of more than two stories; and as there is far more than enough work for everybody, there need be no poverty.

The Anglican Cathedral is a fine wooden building, the outside painted red, while inside, the wood panelling from floor to ceiling is beautifully polished and left absolutely plain. It is just a hundred years since the Rev. Samuel Marsden and his helpers preached Christianity to the Maoris, and most of them are now at least nominal Christians, and they have all given up cannibalism.

Auckland has a very good museum and two picture galleries.

The museum has a magnificent Maori war canoe with exquisitively carved prow; parts of carved or painted houses; and a complete specimen of a Maori dwelling-house made of native bulrush, the long brown leaves packed closely together both for roof and walls, and fastened securely to a framework of wood. A large number of the exhibits, including most of the native weapons—clubs of stone, greenstone or wood, stone axe-heads and wooden spears—were given by Sir George Grey, who was for many years Governor of New Zealand.

There are many specimens of more peaceful implements: fish-hooks made of bone or of glittering "pawa" shell; carved canoe balers, like large wooden slippers; also several fishing-nets. You see a large wicker birdcage of Maori workmanship, and a number of calabashes for holding water; these latter are made out of gourds, and the gourds were originally brought by the Maoris in their canoes from Hawaika. There is a quantity of kauri gum, and many ornaments made from it—all a clear yellow amber colour.

In the art galleries are pictures both by English and New Zealand artists—some of England, Italy or the Mediterranean, others of New Zealand subjects. One of the most striking represents the coming of the Maoris in the Arawa Canoe—supposed to have been in the fourteenth century. The coast of the new country is shown as a distant, blue headland; on the green sea is the brown canoe, crammed with swarthy, brown bodies in the last stages of exhaustion; some of the men able to point out the land, and some looking eagerly, others too weary to care. How men provided with only frail wooden canoes ever dared to leave their homes in some far northern island of the Pacific seems an almost incredible venture of faith: and that they actually voyaged safely for several hundred miles, and in the end found "Ao Tea Roa"—the Land of the Long White Cloud—as they poetically called their new home, is more astonishing still.

Goldie, a New Zealand artist, has very arresting portraits of Maoris. One picture is called "Memories," and shows an old Maori woman brooding over the past glories of her race; the whole face is instinct with thought and feeling, the brown eyes downcast, the skin wrinkled, blue tattoo markings are very plain on the chin, the hair is grey and abundant, and in her ears are long greenstone earrings. The second picture is of a man—a fine type of warrior and cannibal, his face tattooed all over in a geometrical pattern, and the lower lip protruding—a sign that he has lived largely on human flesh. Yet another portrait is of a young and handsome girl, with dark hair and eyes, full red lips, and a clear, brown complexion.

From Auckland, I took a journey of over a hundred miles, in search of a kauri pine forest. The kauri is the king of the New Zealand forest trees and takes a thousand years to come to maturity. It is found only in the northern half of the North Island. Through the kindness of the Auckland Tourist Bureau and the Kauri Timber Company, special arrangements were made for me to see some forests, on the south-east of Auckland, where the trees are now being felled.

I had first a train journey of six hours. The train ran through a level country of swamps alternating with stretches of bracken and manuka scrub, with here and there uncut patches of forest, to the small town of Te Aroha. Here I stayed for the night.

I spent my spare time in climbing half-way up a little, wooded hill behind the town, and from this point gained a glorious view. On the one side lay the blue Hauraki Gulf, shimmering under golden sunset rays; and on the other stretched a great plain, through which wound a blue river, to lose itself in the far distance; and beyond the furthest gleam of the river, with the clear blue sky for background, stood a high, bush-covered mountain, glowing with soft rose-colour as the sun went down.

Next morning I went on again for another hour and a half, and was met on the platform of a tiny country station by the local manager for the Kauri Timber Company. He took me to a curious conveyance strongly built of wood, drawn by a pony and running on tramway lines—a most convenient carriage; for when it was necessary to pass a timber truck, the wheels were taken off the lines, and when the truck had gone by they were put on again. In this carriage we drove for nine miles right into the heart of the bush. We went first through partially cleared country, with a few scattered homesteads; then past bush from which the kauri has been cut, and through acres of which forest fires have swept, leaving bare hillsides and blackened stumps. Here we saw the canvas tents of gum-diggers, who spend their days in searching for gum left many years ago by kauris long since dead. The men are usually Austrians from Croatia, and, I was told, a fine set of people. They probe the ground with long iron rods, and when the point of the rod sticks to gum they begin to dig, and often are successful in digging up huge blocks of clear yellow gum, which they sell at a good price. The gum is either turned into varnish, or used, like European amber, for ornaments.

Growing among magnificent bush of beeches, ratas, red pines and other trees, we saw at last the precious kauri pine—some small trees no thicker than a man's arm, and others giants of twenty feet in girth. The full-grown kauri has a clean, straight trunk of sixty to a hundred feet without a branch; and then a massive head of stout branches stretching out on all sides for another sixty feet, and bearing thick tufts of small green leaves, growing very close together on their stems. The bark is the prettiest colour—pearly grey mottled with pink. We could hear the sound of axes hammering some distance away. After a picnic lunch at the manager's hut, the manager took me over a rough bridge of kauris thrown from side to side of a swift-flowing stream, and then along the edge of a deep trough of yellow mud and on through the forest, until we found men at work among the kauri pines. Some of them were fixing an iron chain round a great log about twelve feet long and six in diameter; when the chain was firmly screwed down, it was attached to an iron rope which ran alongside the mud-trough and across the creek to the engine-house. A shrill whistle was sounded, the engine set in motion, and the log, with a mighty heave, began to move. At turning corners it required great care from the bushmen, and at last it ploughed its way safely through the mud, and was brought quietly to rest by the engine house. Kauri timber is excellent for all purposes of building and furniture, and is now being rapidly cut down; in another twenty years or so, except for scattered trees in inaccessible places, very few will be left.

On my way back to Auckland—a different journey by rail and steamer—a friend had arranged for me to be shown over a gold-mine. Accordingly, I stopped at Thames, a small town nestling under green hills beside a broad estuary at the mouth of the Thames River. The clerk at the booking-office kindly rang up a taxi for me, and I was then driven through the town to the Watchman Mine. To reach the mine, I was taken half-way up one of the hills to the entrance of the mine—a large, roughly-cut hole, with a passage running straight into the hill.

From outside the entrance the view was a splendid one—I looked down on the town beneath and the wide river-mouth, which on the far side is bounded by irregular hills. I could see too for many miles up the Thames Valley—a wide, open plain, at present almost uncultivated, but destined one day to be rich in dairy farms and grain—and towards the head of the valley rose distant blue hills. So often in New Zealand you see this combination of plain and river and distant mountains, all fresh and unspoilt in the bright sunshine and clear atmosphere of a land where smoking factories are rare and fogs unknown.

The mine itself I found to be a succession of dry, dark passages, through which we walked, holding lighted candles. The mine is most scientifically worked. The direction of the gold-bearing reefs is ascertained by experts, and the quartz, in which the gold lies buried, is blasted by dynamite. The quartz is next taken in trucks on a wonderful aerial tramway to a thoroughly up-to-date battery in the valley below. Here the quartz is crushed and mixed with water, and the mud is then treated with cyanide of potassium, which, after separating the gold, deposits it on zinc shavings.

This sort of gold-mining seemed to me a very terrible occupation, when I heard that the miners often get killed through an unexpected explosion of dynamite; and even if the dynamite leaves them unscathed, after working a certain number of years, they get "miners' complaint," and die, choked with dust.

I sailed from Auckland for Sydney on a sunny July day in New Zealand's mid-winter, very sorry to leave such a beautiful country, and the many friends who had done everything in their power to make my visit a pleasant one.

Lector House believes that a society develops through a two-fold approach of continuous learning and adaptation, which is derived from the study of classic literary works spread across the historic timeline of literature records. Therefore, we aim at reviving, repairing and redeveloping all those inaccessible or damaged but historically as well as culturally important literature across subjects so that the future generations may have an opportunity to study and learn from past works to embark upon a journey of creating a better future.

This book is a result of an effort made by Lector House towards making a contribution to the preservation and repair of original ancient works which might hold historical significance to the approach of continuous learning across subjects.

HAPPY READING & LEARNING!

LECTOR HOUSE
LECTOR HOUSE LLP
E-MAIL: lectorpublishing@gmail.com